Cambridge Elements

Elements in Political Economy
edited by
David Stasavage
New York University

DEMOCRACY IN TROUBLE

*Democratic Resilience and Breakdown
from 1900 to 2022*

Myles Williamson
The University of Alabama

Christopher Akor
The University of Alabama

Amanda B. Edgell
The University of Alabama

CAMBRIDGE
UNIVERSITY PRESS

Shaftesbury Road, Cambridge CB2 8EA, United Kingdom

One Liberty Plaza, 20th Floor, New York, NY 10006, USA

477 Williamstown Road, Port Melbourne, VIC 3207, Australia

314–321, 3rd Floor, Plot 3, Splendor Forum, Jasola District Centre,
New Delhi – 110025, India

103 Penang Road, #05–06/07, Visioncrest Commercial, Singapore 238467

Cambridge University Press is part of Cambridge University Press & Assessment,
a department of the University of Cambridge.

We share the University's mission to contribute to society through the pursuit of
education, learning and research at the highest international levels of excellence.

www.cambridge.org
Information on this title: www.cambridge.org/9781009462204

DOI: 10.1017/9781009462181

First published 2024

A catalogue record for this publication is available from the British Library.

ISBN 978-1-009-46220-4 Hardback
ISBN 978-1-009-46221-1 Paperback
ISSN 2398-4031 (online)
ISSN 2514-3816 (print)

An online appendix can be found at www.cambridge.org/Williamson-Akor-Edgell

Democracy in Trouble

Democratic Resilience and Breakdown from 1900 to 2022

Elements in Political Economy

DOI: 10.1017/9781009462181
First published online: December 2024

Myles Williamson
The University of Alabama

Christopher Akor
The University of Alabama

Amanda B. Edgell
The University of Alabama

Author for correspondence: Amanda B. Edgell, abedgell@ua.edu

Abstract: This Element investigates the process of executive aggrandizement to identify factors associated with democratic resilience. The focus is on five democracies that showed resilience in the face of incumbent-led autocratization. To understand how these cases survived, they are paired with similar cases where incumbents successfully dismantled democracy from within. Through structured focused comparisons, insights into how the process of executive aggrandizement unfolds are provided by our inductive exercise. The case narratives reveal similar patterns, with incumbents often targeting the media, civil society, and judiciary and using shared tactics to weaken democratic institutions. Where democracies survived, anti-democratic incumbents made critical errors, including major policy blunders and miscalculations, which ultimately cost them their positions and allowed democracy to rebound. Where democracy broke down, incumbents were largely able to avoid or mitigate such errors, often through ethnopopulist appeals.

Keywords: democratic resilience, democratic backsliding, executive aggrandizement, democratic breakdown, democratic survival

ISBNs: 9781009462204 (HB), 9781009462211 (PB), 9781009462181 (OC)
ISSNs: 2398-4031 (online), 2514-3816 (print)

Contents

An online appendix can be found at
www.cambridge.org/Williamson-Akor-Edgell

1 Introduction

In the late-2000s, South Korea's democracy was in trouble. After coming to power in 2008, President Lee Myung-bak attacked civil liberties, repressed the opposition, and restricted media freedoms. Around this time, Hungary also began experiencing threats to its democracy from Viktor Orbán and his conservative Fidesz party. After taking power in 2010, Orbán weakened judicial institutions, changed the electoral rules, and repressed civil liberties. According to data from the Varieties of Democracy (V-Dem) project, South Korea and Hungary had similar levels of democracy and both countries had been democratic for over 15 years when their elected leaders started to undermine democracy from within (Coppedge et al., 2023; Edgell et al., 2023).[1] Despite these similarities, however, South Korea's democracy has bounced back, whereas Hungary's broke down in 2018 according to data from the V-Dem institute (Edgell et al., 2023).

Previous research shows that "democracy's near misses" like South Korea demand special attention and are quite rare (Ginsburg & Huq, 2018, 17). For example, Boese et al. (2021) find that democracies survived in less than one-quarter of the episodes of democratic backsliding from 1900 to 2019. How did the process unfold in these "near misses" when compared to episodes where democracy broke down? Can these endogenous processes help us draw insights about how democracies survive when faced with an existential threat from within?

In this Element, we investigate the process of executive aggrandizement – or the deliberate and gradual dismantling of democratic institutions by a democratically elected executive (Bermeo, 2016). Using structured focused comparisons, we describe the process of incumbent-driven autocratization and uncover factors associated with democratic resilience – or the ability for a democracy to sustain itself when faced with serious challenges from within. Drawing on the Episodes of Regime Transformation dataset (ERT) produced by the V-Dem Institute, we identify five democracies that showed resilience in the face of incumbent-led autocratization. We match each of these "near misses" with a similar case where democracy broke down (Eckstein, 1975). Our case narratives reveal insights into the process of executive aggrandizement and potential mechanisms that could explain democratic resilience.

Our descriptive findings reveal strikingly similar patterns of executive aggrandizement across the cases, despite their different starting values

---

[1] Their scores on the electoral democracy index (EDI) were 0.84 and 0.86, respectively (Coppedge et al., 2023). Duration of democratic spells based on coding of regimes in the Episodes of Regime Transformation (ERT) dataset (Edgell et al., 2023).

and outcomes. In all our cases, incumbents eroded democracy by restricting and manipulating the media environment and civil society spaces. Executives in many of the cases also attempted or successfully made constitutional changes that undermined the democratic process. Likewise, several cases featured instances where the incumbents packed key accountability institutions with personal and party loyalists. All of this suggests that incumbents follow a similar playbook when they engage in executive aggrandizement, using the shield of legality to chip away at democracy from the inside (also see Sato et al., 2022).

Building from these insights and our additional findings from the case narratives, we present tentative conclusions about the factors that appear to contribute to democratic resilience. Most notably, we find that in each case where democracy survived, anti-democratic incumbents made critical errors, including major policy blunders and miscalculations, which ultimately cost them their positions and allowed democracy to rebound. Economic mismanagement and high-level corruption prompted anti-government demonstrations, which eroded the legitimacy and strength of the executive. When faced with this reputational crisis, incumbents made additional errors in how they responded, ultimately leading to the executive's removal through elections or impeachment. In particular, executives in all the "near misses" overestimated their popular support and underestimated institutional checks on their authority. By contrast, where democracy broke down, we find that incumbents used divisive populist rhetoric to scapegoat and avoid blame for their actions, thereby circumventing or avoiding a crisis. Thus, democratic survival may often rest on the opportunities and incentives for would-be autocrats to create a common enemy – such as through xenophobia or culture wars – that stokes fear and allows incumbents to divert blame.

We are not the first to investigate democratic resilience in cases experiencing democratic decline. For example, Haggard and Kaufman (2021) analyze democratic backsliding in sixteen countries, arguing that polarization and party realignment lead to the election of autocrats who then use parliamentary majorities to dismantle democracy from within. Unlike Haggard and Kaufman (2021), we are not interested in explaining *why* democratic backsliding occurs; instead, we are interested in *how* democracies survive once backsliding begins. This makes our empirical puzzle more in line with work by Laebens and Lührmann (2021) and Ginsburg and Huq (2018), which focus on cases where democracy survived substantial backsliding. Furthermore, we leverage information from similar cases where democracy broke down, using within- and between-case structured-focused comparisons that avoids selecting on the dependent variable. As such, our research aligns more closely with recent studies by Cleary and Öztürk (2022) and Gamboa (2022); however, we take a more inductively driven approach rather than focusing specifically on opposition strategies.

While our approach has several advantages, we recognize the inherent limitations in small-N research. Our conclusions about the processes and potential factors that affect the outcomes of executive aggrandizement are based on nine cases, most of which occurred fairly recently. Our results may be affected by the choice of thresholds used to construct our sample of episodes, something we discuss in the methodology below and the online appendix. Finally, while we approached the research from an exploratory and inductive perspective with few explicit assumptions about the cases, processes, and outcomes, we cannot discount the potential for implicit biases or that we simply overlooked important details due to underreporting on certain events. Ultimately, we provide tentative conclusions about the processes and outcomes as they occurred in the particular set of cases based on the available evidence we could bring to bear. Future research may expand upon our findings through additional cases and new evidence to assess whether our conclusions hold in a more general sense.

In the following sections, we provide a brief overview of the literature on executive aggrandizement and democratic resilience, including how we conceptualized these terms for this study. Afterward, we explain our methodology for selecting and analyzing cases using matching methods and comparative historical analysis. Then we present detailed case narratives for our five comparative case studies. We conclude by summarizing our core findings about the nature of executive aggrandizement and offer insights into the implications of these findings, particularly for future research and policy interventions.

2 Executive Aggrandizement and Democratic Resilience

The tendency toward more gradual erosion of democracy from within, as opposed to the more radical breakdowns due to coups and autogolpes, has attracted broad interest from the scholarly community. Elected leaders use their power to gradually dismantle democratic institutions and practices from within through a process known as executive aggrandizement (Bermeo, 2016), which can lead to the "collapse of the separation of powers" and a narrowing of fundamental freedoms required for democracy to function (Haggard & Kaufman, 2021). Thus, executive aggrandizement is a specific type of autocratization (Lührmann & Lindberg, 2019), which occurs when a regime experiences substantial declines in the quality of the institutions and practices associated with democracy through deliberate actions by the executive leadership. For example, after the Law and Justice Party in Poland stoked top-down polarization to gain power, it pushed through constitutional changes to reduce electoral competition (Tworzecki, 2019). In Turkey, President Recep Tayyip Erdoğan has repressed the media into a "dominant singular political narrative" (Över, 2021, 343). And in Venezuela, Hugo Chávez manipulated electoral practices to disable the opposition (Corrales, 2020). We add to a growing body of literature that explains democratic resilience in the face of these pressures.

Before proceeding, it is important to clarify what we mean by democracy and democratic resilience. Drawing on Dahl (1971, 2), we consider democracy to be a political system that is "completely or almost completely responsive to all its citizens." As such, democracies have a set of institutions and practices that facilitate broad participation and contestation necessary to ensure that citizens can hold those in power accountable and freely and fairly express their preferences about who governs. In particular, democracies respect freedom of association and expression, provide access to alternative sources of information, have expansive suffrage and standing rights, hold free and fair elections for major public offices (e.g., legislature, executive), and have institutional checks to ensure that policies reflect the public's preferences (Dahl, 1971).

We approach democracy as a matter of degree and difference in kind (Sartori, 1970). In other words, political regimes vary in their level of *democraticness* and can also be dichotomized into mutually exclusive categories labeled *democracy* and *autocracy*. The quality of democracy in any given political system falls along a range, depending on the degree to which the regime incorporates democratic institutions and practices. At the same time, we can also determine a point where the quality of democracy is sufficient to say that a particular regime is democratic.

Executive aggrandizement is a heterogeneous and uncertain process. Anti-democratic leaders undermine various institutions and practices at different stages, aiming to evade detection and counter-mobilization (Haggard & Kaufman, 2021). As a result, more minimalist definitions of democracy – for example Schumpeter (1942) – would overlook many cases precisely because executive aggrandizement "makes elections less competitive without entirely undermining the electoral mechanism" and "restricts participation without explicitly abolishing norms of universal franchise" (Waldner & Lust, 2018, 95).

In general, democratic resilience is the ability for a democracy to withstand stressors or rebound after facing a threat from within. Linz (1978, 87) refers to this as reequilibration or "a political process that, after a crisis that has seriously threatened the continuity and stability of the basic democratic political mechanisms, results in their continued existence at the same or higher levels of democratic legitimacy, efficacy, and effectiveness." In other words, democratic resilience manifests empirically as a potential outcome of executive aggrandizement, namely survival rather than breakdown.[2]

Interest in democratic resilience has grown during the current wave of autocratization (Lührmann & Lindberg, 2019), largely mirroring the interest in democratic consolidation that emerged during the third wave of democratization (Huntington, 1993). Democratic consolidation refers to the condition where democracy has no viable alternatives and is considered the "only game in town" (Linz & Stepan, 1996, 15). For some, consolidation is the final phase of democratization, whereby democracy becomes so embedded that it is highly difficult to dislodge (Huntington, 1993). By contrast, democratic resilience focuses primarily on current and past cases, seeking to identify factors that facilitate democratic survival, particularly once autocratization has begun. Resilience is a trait that democracies exhibit at a particular time; it can ebb and flow and does not always manifest at a particular stage of democratic development or as an inherent characteristic of the regime. In other words, we cannot speak of resilient democracies in the same way we might speak about consolidated democracies (on this point, also see Boese et al., 2021). Rather, while all consolidated democracies exhibit high democratic resilience, some unconsolidated democracies may also be resilient at a given point in time depending on the circumstances.

The literature provides several insights into the factors that may help explain democratic resilience. Early work by Linz (1978, 88) stresses the importance of elites, arguing that democratic resilience is more likely when a pro-democratic opposition can neutralize threats from an anti-democratic one. Thus, we might expect that elite actors play important roles as democratic spoilers or protectors, depending on whether they act as loyal, semi-loyal, or disloyal opposition to the regime. Recent work supports this argument, showing that under conditions of executive aggrandizement if the opposition attempts to remove the incumbent through irregular means rather than waiting it out until the next election, this is likely to result in a democratic breakdown (Cleary & Öztürk, 2022). Evidence from Boese et al. (2021) and Lührmann (2021) suggests that legislatures can do very little to halt backsliding once it has started, absent other contextual factors such as a major scandal (e.g., South Korea). Meanwhile, a broader set of non-elected actors, including the judiciary, bureaucracy, military, and party elites, may help to explain democracy's "near misses" (Ginsburg & Huq, 2018).

---

[2] Here we focus on resilience once autocratization is underway; however, democracies may also show resilience by avoiding autocratization altogether, something Boese et al. (2021) refer to as "onset resilience."

In particular, evidence suggests that the judiciary may play a crucial role in democratic survival (Boese et al., 2021; Gibler & Randazzo, 2011; Reenock et al., 2013).

Structural conditions may also matter. Economic development remains one of the most important predictors of democratic survival in the literature (Lipset, 1959; Przeworski & Limongi, 1997), and recent work reiterates its importance for sustaining democracy once autocratization begins (Brownlee & Miao, 2022). Finally, democratic resilience is likely to be self-reinforcing because countries with more democratic experience and those in a more democratic neighborhood are less likely to break down (Boese et al., 2021).

We build on these studies by directly addressing the question of democratic resilience from the viewpoint of cases where executive aggrandizement posed a real threat to democracy. While previous studies provide valuable insights into the survival of democracy more generally, only recently have scholars investigated democratic resilience among a sample of cases where democratic erosion occurred (Boese et al., 2021; Cleary & Öztürk, 2022; Gamboa, 2022; Ginsburg & Huq, 2018; Laebens & Lührmann, 2021). This distinction is important because some democracies (e.g., Sweden) are very stable, whereas others experience a serious threat from within but survive (e.g., South Korea from 2008 to 2014). A binary approach to democratic survival treats all cases of democratic survival the same. By identifying periods of executive aggrandizement, we can distinguish between stable democracies and those that faced an existential threat from within. This allows us to engage in process tracing to understand better how executive aggrandizement unfolds and to identify factors that could help to explain when it results in democratic breakdown or survival.

3 Methodology

Our approach is akin to analytical induction with the goal of theory building (George, 1979). More specifically, we employ the method of structured focused comparison developed by George and Bennett (2005). This method relies upon careful case selection from the universe of possible cases, a well-defined research objective, and a standardized set of questions that can be applied to each case. Importantly, we follow advice from Lijphart (1971, 686) that "[a]ll cases should, of course, be selected systematically, and the scientific search should be aimed at probabilistic, not universal, generalizations." The authors had little prior knowledge of these cases before beginning this project and, while implicit biases are always possible, did not set out to prove any particular theory. Thus, our inductive approach has the benefit of allowing us to engage with historical material from the cases without any explicit prior expectations about how the process unfolded or why a particular outcome occurred.

Ultimately, this means that our research design rests upon a small sample of cases from which we can draw bounded observations about the process and outcomes of executive aggrandizement. Our observations are bounded in the sense that they rely upon the accuracy of primary and secondary sources available to us at the time we conducted this research. Our findings are also bounded because they reflect our assessment of historical events, including the actions taken by leaders during each episode and how these may have affected the outcome. As with any inductive research design, additional cases or the discovery of new historical evidence within the same cases could lead to adjustments in our findings or call into question their scope conditions. We also acknowledge that our implicit biases may unavoidably influence our assessment of historical events, and a different set of authors may come to different conclusions using the same cases and sources. Nevertheless, we hope that our bounded observations of these cases are beneficial for theory-building about democratic resilience.

3.1 Identifying Cases of Executive Aggrandizement

To identify our universe of cases, we use the Episodes of Regime Transformation (ERT) dataset produced by the V-Dem Institute (Edgell et al., 2023; Maerz et al., 2023). The ERT leverages the world's largest dataset on democracy to classify country years into episodes of autocratization and democratization. Drawing on Dahl's (1971) definition of polyarchy, the ERT uses the V-Dem Electoral Democracy Index (EDI) to assess aggregate changes in democracy levels over time. This index combines twenty-four subjective indicators of democratic institutions and practices from the V-Dem annual expert survey with additional indicators of suffrage and elected officials hard-coded by the V-Dem Institute research team.[3]

Autocratization denotes a substantial decline in attributes associated with democracy (also see Lührmann & Lindberg, 2019). We use this term interchangeably with "democratic backsliding," which has become the vernacular in recent years (Waldner & Lust, 2018).[4] In the ERT dataset, *episodes* of autocratization occur when a country experiences an annual decline of 0.01 or more

---

[3] For more on the aggregation rules, see the V-Dem Codebook (Coppedge et al., 2023).

[4] Although, we also acknowledge that some, including several of the ERT authors, take issue with this terminology. See Wilson et al. (2024).

on the EDI, with a total decline of at least 0.10 for the entire episode. The episode ends when the country registers a substantial increase in the EDI of at least 0.03 in a given year or 0.10 over a five-year period.

We use the regime types and outcomes coded in the ERT to establish whether each episode resulted in democratic survival or breakdown. The ERT identifies democratic regimes using three necessary and jointly sufficient criteria: (1) the country scores higher than 0.50 on the EDI, (2) it holds multiparty elections for the legislature and executive that are determined to be sufficiently free and fair, and (3) elected officials assumed office after the election.[5] Country-years failing to meet one or more of these criteria are considered autocratic regimes. Accordingly, democratic breakdown occurs when the country no longer meets one or more of the necessary conditions for democracy.[6]

Based on previous research (Boese et al., 2021) and the ERT data, we know that democracies are highly resilient to the *onset of backsliding*; however, once this process begins, democracies rarely survive. This empirical observation largely motivates our analysis. The ERT identifies ninety-two episodes of autocratization that originated in democracies. As of December 2022, seventeen of these episodes were ongoing in countries where democracy had not (yet) broken down. Therefore, we exclude these censored cases from our analysis because the outcome is unknown. This leaves us with seventy-five possible episodes to select from in our universe of cases. Most of these episodes resulted in a democratic breakdown, with only ten out of seventy-five in our sample surviving (about 13 percent).

Because we are interested in resilience to executive aggrandizement, we limit the sample to episodes where we can be reasonably certain autocratization was driven by democratically elected incumbents rather than outside forces. We exclude episodes in the ERT lasting less than three years and where the primary trigger for the episode is a sudden illegal seizure of power, for example, by military coup or autogolpe. We use data on successful military coups compiled by Albrecht et al. (2021, 2022) and V-Dem data capturing whether elections are on schedule and whether the legislature has been closed down or

---

[5] Criteria (2) is based on a minimum score of "2" on V-Dem expert-coded indicators for multiparty elections *v2elmulpar_osp* and free and fair elections *v2elfrfair_osp*. This comes directly from the Regimes of the World (RoW) measure developed by Lührmann et al. (2018). The ERT adds criteria (3) that elections must be held after which officials assume office, based on a minimum score of "2" the V-Dem expert-coded variable *v2elasmoff_ord*. For more detailed information, see Maerz et al. (2023) and Edgell et al. (2023).

[6] More specifically, breakdowns occur when (1) the country no longer has elections for the legislature and the executive, (2) the country falls below 0.50 on the EDI and holds an election that is not free and fair, or (3) the country remains below 0.50 on the EDI for five years or more.

aborted (Coppedge et al., 2023). If any of these events occur within the pre-episode year or the first year of the episode, we consider an illegal power grab the primary means of autocratization rather than executive aggrandizement and, therefore, exclude the case.

Using these additional scope conditions, we excluded forty episodes that lasted less than three years (see online appendix, Table 3). Nine of these episodes started via a coup, and eleven others experienced a suspension of the legislature or electoral calendar without a coup. After eliminating very short episodes and those driven by outside forces, we were left with thirty-five episodes characterized by executive aggrandizement, including seven where democracy survived and twenty-eight possible matches where democracy broke down. Based on historical evidence, however, we also decided to exclude Lesotho (2015–2017) and Moldova (2013–2017) because they did not meet our criteria for executive aggrandizement. Lesotho's episode was prompted by an attempted autogolpe, followed by an attempted military coup. Moldova, on the other hand, represents a case of state capture by corrupt oligarchic politicians (also see Laebens & Lührmann, 2021). We provide longer historical narratives for these cases in our online appendix for reference.

The default coding rules for the ERT rely on a set of thresholds selected through a lengthy and iterative process designed to maximize face validity while detecting autocratization episodes from their earliest stages (Maerz et al., 2023). Other studies use similar parameters to measure episodes, such as Haggard and Kaufman (2021), making it easier to compare our findings to other works in the literature. At the same time, we acknowledge that thresholds on a continuous scale introduce an element of arbitrariness and that changes to these thresholds may affect our sample of episodes.

Concerns over false positives might lead some to question whether 0.10 is substantial enough to denote autocratization (Tomini, 2021). Research by Pelke and Croissant (2021), however, shows that 0.10 is a face-valid threshold for substantial autocratization. Increasing this threshold would lead to fewer episodes and is likely to introduce false negatives into the sample. At the same time, Pelke and Croissant (2021) also emphasize the importance of limiting episodes to "significant" changes using the uncertainty interval from the V-Dem measurement model (also see Lott, 2023). Only twelve (out of 245) autocratization episodes in the ERT show overall changes within the uncertainty boundaries from the V-Dem measurement model, and five of these were ongoing as of December 2022, making it unclear whether they will eventually show "significant" changes. Our selection criteria – particularly the requirement that episodes last longer than two years – eliminates most of these "insignificant" episodes from the universe of cases.

Bulgaria (2001–2018) remains in our sample despite the uncertainty boundaries of its lowest EDI value and its pre-episode EDI overlapping by about 0.022. After reviewing the case, however, we find evidence of substantial backsliding due to executive aggrandizement, particularly when it comes to media freedoms and the rule of law. Indeed, the case experienced a 15 percent drop in the EDI from its pre-episode value to its lowest point. We address this in more detail in Section 5.

In the online appendix, we discuss how our sample of episodes changes when we make other adjustments to the default parameters of the ERT. As one might expect, decreasing the threshold for total decline to 0.05 increases the number of episodes in the sample, but this also introduces more potential "false positives" as gauged by overlapping uncertainty boundaries on the EDI from the pre-episode year and the final year of the episode. Increasing the parameter that accounts for the start of an episode and whether it remains ongoing (i.e., from 0.01 to 0.05), also reduces the face validity of the episodes. By setting a very high threshold for inclusion and continuation, most episodes are only one year long, and several well-known cases of democratic breakdown due to executive aggrandizement occur outside of episodes (e.g., Turkey under Erdoğan and Venezuela under Chávez).

3.2 Selecting Matched Cases

The identification strategy above left us with five cases where democracies survived episodes of executive aggrandizement: India (1971–1975), Bulgaria (2001–2018), Ecuador (2007–2013), South Korea (2008–2014), and Slovenia (2011–2021). Our research focuses on qualitatively explaining these "extreme" cases through exploratory and inductively driven historical process tracing. These cases are considered extreme because they have an unusual value on the dependent variable (Y), that is, survival. Extreme cases are most useful for exploratory open-ended probes; however, using them to make conclusions about a broader population is problematic due to known issues with selecting on the dependent variable (Seawright & Gerring, 2008). To avoid this problem, we employ a combined within and between-case research design. We draw on evidence from democracies that survived, like South Korea, and match them with similar cases where democracy broke down, like Hungary. By comparing the historical processes that unfolded in democracies that survived to those that occurred in similar democracies that broke down, we hope to draw insights into the processes of executive aggrandizement and to uncover potential explanations for democratic resilience.

Table 1 Selected cases of executive aggrandizement

Democratic resilience			Democratic breakdown			
Country	Years	EDI	Country	Years	EDI	Distance
India (IND)	1971–1975	0.662	Sri Lanka (LKA)	1970–1983	0.664	0.009
Bulgaria (BGR)	2001–2018	0.722	India (IND)	2000–2017	0.743	0.023
Ecuador (ECU)	2007–2013	0.703	Turkey (TUR)	2005–2013	0.677	0.031
S. Korea (KOR)	2008–2014	0.846	Hungary (HUN)	2006–2018	0.853	0.018
Slovenia (SVN)	2011–2021	0.872	Hungary (HUN)	2006–2018	0.853	0.046

To select cases for comparison, we focus on temporal proximity and starting levels of democracy. This allows us to control for the relative quality of democracy before autocratization started, which might influence the likelihood that a particular democracy is resilient. It also ensures that the matched episodes occurred in a similar time period, thereby controlling for potential temporal effects and global events. In the online appendix, we discuss the matching process in more detail and several alternative matching formulae. We calculated the closest match based on Euclidian distance. Before doing so, we feature rescaled the year values to a 0-1 interval so that they do not outweigh the values of EDI using a simple max-min method. Then we used the Euclidian distance formula to find the nearest match:

$$\text{Distance} = \sqrt{(x1 - x2)^2 + (y1 - y2)^2} \tag{3.1}$$

where x is the feature re-scaled onset year, and y is the starting EDI value for the resilient (1) and non-resilient (2) episodes. We calculated the distance between the resilient episodes and all non-resilient episodes in the sample. The non-resilient episode that has the shortest distance is considered the closest match.

Table 1 and Figure 1 report the five democracies that survived and their closest match that broke down. Only one pair of cases in our study occurred before the third wave of autocratization: India (1971–1975) and Sri Lanka (1970–1983).[7] The remaining episodes occurred during the twenty-first century. Fortuitously, our matching exercise includes some of the most high-profile cases of executive aggrandizement in recent years. A more recent episode in India (2000–2017) appears as a match for Bulgaria (2001–2018). While not the main focus of our analysis, this allows us to draw within-case comparisons

---

[7] Finland (1939–1940), Turkey (1970–1971), and Suriname (1975) also appear as episodes where democracies survived in the ERT (v13). However, we eliminated these from our analysis because the episodes lasted less than three years and qualitative evidence shows they are not the result of executive aggrandizement. We discuss these cases briefly in our online appendix.

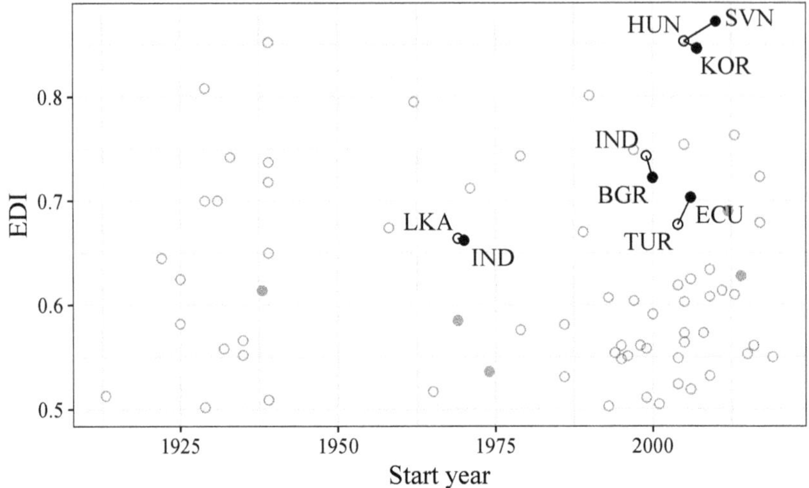

○ democratic breakdown   ● democratic resilience

Figure 1 Selected cases of executive aggrandizement matched based on minimum Euclidian distance for starting year and starting value on the EDI. Also shown (in lighter shading) are all other episodes of autocratization in democracies found in the ERT (v13) dataset.

for India between the earlier episode under Indira Gandhi and the contemporary episode leading to breakdown under Narendra Modi (see Section 5). Meanwhile, Ecuador's episode under Rafael Correa (2007–2013) matches with Turkey under Recep Tayyip Erdoğan (2005–2013). Finally, both South Korea (2008–2014) and Slovenia (2011–2021) match with Hungary (2006–2018), facilitating a three-way comparison of these cases in Section 7.

By capturing long-run processes from their earliest stages, the ERT dataset allows us to identify episodes for process tracing. This approach emphasizes contingent processes of regime transformation that may span several years, rather than annual changes, upturns, or downturns (e.g., Coppedge et al., 2022; Teorell, 2010). After identifying each set of cases, we structured our comparisons by developing a set of general questions to apply to each case, all within our overall objective of understanding how democratic resilience emerges. These questions included:

- *Background*: What was the historical context within which the episode began?
- *The episode*: What was the nature of backsliding throughout the episode? What formal and informal steps did the executive take to undermine democracy? Which democratic institutions, norms, and practices did they target, and in what order?

- *Aftermath*: How did the episode end? What events occurred that facilitated the end of the episode? What actors were involved? What was the aftermath of the episode like?

Based on a survey of historical references, we constructed a narrative of each case focusing specifically upon answering these questions. We reproduce these narratives in the sections that follow. This approach allows us to piece together the story of executive aggrandizement and draw insights into the factors that help explain the outcome in each case. In Section 8, we elaborate more on the findings across the cases and suggest avenues for future research.

4 India and Sri Lanka

Based on levels of economic development (Boix, 2011; Brownlee & Miao, 2022; Lijphart, 1977; Lipset, 1959; Przeworski, 2000; Przeworski & Limongi, 1997) and ethnic heterogeneity (Dahl, 1971; Horowitz, 2000; Rabushka, 1972; Welsh, 1993) – the chances of democracy in India and Sri Lanka were low at the time of independence. These might be considered "hard places" for democracy (Mainwaring & Masoud, 2022). Both were poor, multi-ethnic countries with dominant and minority groups trying to assert their rights. Yet somehow, India and Sri Lanka transitioned to democracy almost immediately after obtaining independence from the British in the late 1940s. By the 1970s, however, executive aggrandizement in both countries threatened these unlikely democratic experiments, as illustrated by the V-Dem EDI in Figure 2. India's democracy survived this episode, while Sri Lanka's did not. What accounts for the differences in the outcome of these two similar South Asian cases?

4.1 India (1971–1975)

4.1.1 Background: Leading up to the Episode

Indira Gandhi, daughter of the first Indian prime minister, Jawaharlal Nehru, came to power in early 1966 after the death of her father's successor, Lal Bahadur Shastri. Encyclopaedia Britannica (2020) describes her as "soft-spoken" with an "attractive personality," which "masked her iron will and autocratic ambition." Gandhi ascended to power with support from the conservative Syndicate faction of the ruling India National Congress, who saw her as both popular and easy to manage (Leepson, 1976). At the time, she was "seen as a truly progressive democrat committed to secular values and acceptable to all minorities" (Mussells, 1980, 59). Yet, throughout her first year in office, the opposition and media ridiculed Gandhi as a Syndicate puppet, openly referring to her as a *goongi gudiya* or "dumb doll" in Hindu (Malhotra, 1989). Everyone clearly underestimated her strength and popularity.

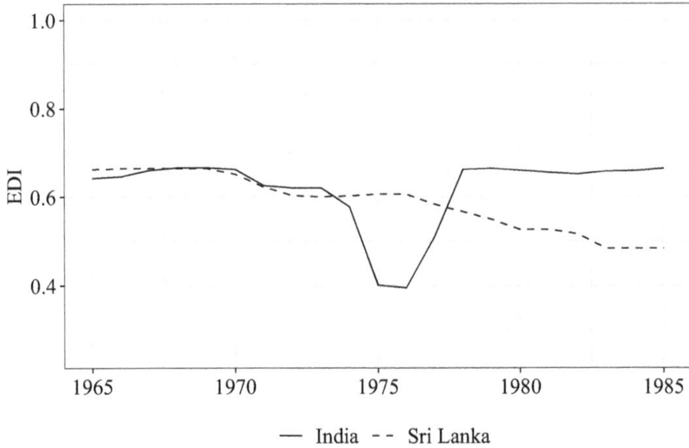

Figure 2 Electoral democracy in India and Sri Lanka, 1965–1985

Gandhi quickly became impatient with the Syndicate's conservative approach and began to exert greater independence. She skillfully adopted a populist rhetoric, portraying herself as "a radical reformer thwarted in her attempts by these 'reactionary' Congress elders" (Mussells, 1980, 56). Throughout the 1967 campaign, Gandhi strategically invoked direct and personal appeals to the people, framing herself as the only politician who really cared about them (Malhotra, 1989). She made good on this rhetoric in 1969 by nationalizing India's fourteen largest banks and forcing out the Deputy Prime Minister and Finance Minister, Morarji Desai, who was aligned with the Syndicate. Then Gandhi boldly helped V. V. Giri win the presidency over the Syndicate-backed candidate Sanjiva Reddy, securing her popularity as someone who stood up for the people by challenging the old guard (Leepson, 1976; Time, 1969). An attempt to expel Gandhi from the party led to a split, with most Congress MPs choosing to side with Gandhi over the Syndicate bloc. This earned Gandhi the nickname *Kali* for the Hindu goddess of destruction (Time, 1969) – a far cry from her *goongi gudiya* title just two years prior.

4.1.2 The Autocratization Episode

When the episode begins, Gandhi had achieved the peak of her popularity. Having won a majority of seats in the 1971 election, she went on to oversee India's resounding victory in a brief war with Pakistan that produced an independent Bangladesh. Thereafter, the 1972 elections saw large majorities for Gandhi's party in most states. As Leepson (1976, 10) observes, "She was supreme in the government, the party, and among the people. Indeed, she was widely thought of by the masses as Durga, the Hindu goddess of war."

Having achieved total control of her party, the parliament, and most states of the Indian federation, Gandhi developed a cult of personality around herself. Access to party leadership and government positions depended upon loyalty to the Prime Minister rather than based on merit or seniority within the party (Mussells, 1980). Corruption and nepotism became widespread within the government, with scandals over dubious contracts, tax evasion, and loan schemes making headlines on a near weekly basis (Baloch, 2021). Gandhi also strategically chipped away at India's democratic institutions through amendments, laws, and decrees while insisting that these actions would preserve and safeguard India's democracy (Henderson, 1979, 947). Throughout her tenure, Gandhi introduced twenty-five constitutional amendments that greatly increased the powers of the prime minister and limited fundamental rights while also circumscribing the powers of the courts (Mussells, 1980).

However, Gandhi was unable to substantially influence the judiciary, which continued to check her excesses. For example, the courts attempted to limit the government's nationalization and land reform program by striking down a constitutional amendment that restricted property rights in 1967. Undeterred, Gandhi's government responded by adopting three constitutional amendments that gave the parliament sweeping powers to alter fundamental rights and limited the court's jurisdiction in property rights cases (Ueda, 2019). In 1973, the courts ruled against these amendments, arguing that the parliament had no power to alter the basic structure of the constitution (Sezgin, 2018). In an attempt to rein in the courts, Gandhi appointed pro-government chief justices in 1973 and 1977, "even though they were not the most senior members of the Supreme Court at the time, superseding more senior judges who had refused to take her side in court cases" (Ueda, 2019, 59).

Gandhi's popularity began to wane by early 1974. High oil prices combined with the nationalization of key industries and government control over essential commodities led to rising inflation, poverty, and unemployment (Leepson, 1976). Anti-government demonstrations grew to a size not seen since the independence period (Plys, 2020). Many of these protests centered in Bihar and Gujarat states, where university students led strikes and demonstrations that often turned violent, including setting fires in university, government, and newspaper offices as well as looting. The far-right Hindu nationalist and far-left Maoist parties were often responsible for these protests (Leepson, 1976). Railway workers also staged a mass strike for twenty days in May 1974, leading to an estimated $1.5 to $2 billion in losses for the Indian economy (Weinraub, 1974).

While initially leaderless, protests eventually coalesced around a single leader – Jayaprakash Narayan (or JP) – "a major national figure with a high reputation for integrity" once considered Nehru's successor (Joshi, 1975, 89). Calling for "total revolution," the JP movement drew support from across the political spectrum, presenting a major challenge to Gandhi's rule despite its ideological incoherence. It pitted Gandhi as an "authoritarian premier against JP; an 'aging people's hero'" (Ankit, 2021, 215). The government labeled the movement "reactionary, subversive, and even 'fascist'" (Joshi, 1975, 90), responding with violent repression that led to untold deaths and arrests in the hundreds of thousands (Plys, 2020; Weinraub, 1974). However, reflecting the growing anger with unemployment, inflation, and corruption, the JP movement quickly spread and evolved to include a cross-section of students, business elites, politicians, and activists. In March 1975, the JP movement led a procession of 500,000 people to the Indian parliament to deliver a list of demands (Baloch, 2021).

The crisis escalated in June 1975 when a court convicted Gandhi of corruption during her 1971 election campaign. Under the law, the conviction invalidated Gandhi's parliamentary election and barred her from holding public office for six years. Gandhi refused to step down and lodged an appeal with the Supreme Court. The ruling emboldened the JP movement, which launched major protests throughout the capital and organized a nationwide civil disobedience campaign calling for Gandhi to resign (R. L. Park, 1975). On the morning of 26 June 1975, Gandhi's government declared a state of emergency, suspending all civil liberties (Leepson, 1976; Sterling, 1975). Officially, she justified the state of emergency as necessary to restore law and order. She blamed the mass demonstrations, particularly the JP movement, for undermining economic progress. Yet, as Plys (2020, 131–132) notes, "the declaration of Emergency did not occur until there was a real threat that risked removing Gandhi from office."

Over the next twenty-one months, India's democracy virtually broke down, and Gandhi ruled by decree.[8] Thousands of opposition supporters across the political spectrum, including from within Gandhi's own party, were arrested (Baloch, 2021). India's Supreme Court validated these detentions when it ruled that the right of habeas corpus could be suspended under a state of emergency (Palmer, 1977). Media restrictions imposed by the government resulted in the expulsion of foreign journalists and widespread censorship

---

[8] The ERT dataset does not count this case as a democratic breakdown because the scores rebounded before elections occurred, and we agree with others who have argued that this case constitutes an "authoritarian interlude" (Mitra, 1992, 9). Most notably, we see the democratic constitution put on hold rather than being abolished and this same institutional arrangement being promptly reinstated in 1977. It would be difficult to argue that the democracy in 1974 was a different regime from the one in 1978.

(Singh, 1980) – with one commentator observing "the Indian press has issued papers that have an 'Alice in Wonderland' appearance: one would think nothing of political note is happening in India, except favorable actions of the Government and successful economic growth (R. L. Park, 1975, 1006)." Meanwhile, the government postponed elections twice, extending the rule of the parliament and insulating Gandhi from vertical accountability through the ballot box (Palmer, 1977).

With major opposition groups banned, most of the opposition lawmakers in prison, and the judiciary severely weakened, Gandhi began changing India's fundamental legal frameworks in a more authoritarian direction. In late 1975, the government pushed through an amendment to the electoral laws that retroactively cleared Gandhi of her criminal conviction (Borders, 1975). Afterward, the courts had no choice but to vacate the sentence. Then, in 1976, Gandhi's government passed sweeping changes to the constitution that restricted civil liberties, reduced the judiciary's review function, and awarded greater power to the Prime Minister. Thus, despite Gandhi's insistence that the Emergency was a temporary inconvenience for national security, observers noted that her behavior suggested she aimed to remake India into a lasting dictatorship (Palmer, 1977).

4.1.3 End of the Episode

Things seemed to be going well for Indira Gandhi. Two good monsoon seasons helped to drive down inflation and India's overall economy improved. In January 1977, she seized on this opportunity and announced that elections would be held in March. To facilitate the poll, Gandhi also agreed to relax some of the Emergency restrictions on media freedom and public meetings and released thousands of opposition members from jail (Hardgrave, 1979). Congress expected to win a large majority due to the good economic conditions and splintered opposition. An electoral victory would legitimize the state of emergency, codify many aspects of it into law, and set Gandhi's son Sanjay up to become the next Prime Minister (Weiner, 1977).

However, Gandhi miscalculated her own popularity. An opposition coalition called the Janata Alliance mounted a successful campaign against the ruling Congress party. They were able to successfully build support among both urban elites disenchanted with the Emergency's draconian measures and rural Indians who had suffered under Gandhi's expansive and often coercive sterilization programs aimed at curbing population growth (Weiner, 1977). Gandhi lost her parliamentary seat, and Congress was roundly defeated. After the election, the Janata Alliance lifted the state of emergency and oversaw the renewal of Indian democracy.

4.2 Sri Lanka (1970–1983)

4.2.1 Background: Leading up to the Episode

Before Sirimavo Bandaranaike emerged as Ceylon's newly elected leader in July 1960, she was largely viewed as a "politically naive, withdrawn, and recently bereaved widow" (Buultjens, 1982, 12). Her unlikely emergence as the world's first woman prime minister came about due to a political vacuum in the left-wing Sri Lanka Freedom Party (SLFP). In September 1959, a Buddhist priest assassinated Bandaranaike's husband, who had founded the SLFP and was then serving as prime minister. Thereafter, the SLFP struggled to identify a new leader, forcing Bandaranaike "to come out of her mourning and save her husband's party from total decay" (Rangnekar, 1960, 373). While Time Magazine warned " that she had not the foggiest idea of how to run a government" (Time, 1960), throughout her time as prime minister, Bandaranaike defied expectations.

In particular, Bandaranaike carried on her husband's legacy with fervor by pushing the Sinhalese national project. The SLFP exploited ethnic divisions in Ceylon, framing them as a "life and death struggle" for the majority Sinhalese against the minority Tamil population (DeVotta, 2002, 86). They perpetuated a colonial myth that the Sinhalese were descendants of a great civilization linked to the Aryan race. The SLFP used this myth to activate a sense of "ethnic entitlement" among Sinhalese voters over the minority Tamil population, who they portrayed as "invaders" (De Silva Wijeyeratne, 1996). Bandaranaike's government imposed Sinhalese as the official state language, requiring that civil servants resign if they could not speak it. This led to protests, followed by a government-imposed state of emergency in the Tamil areas of the country. While these programs suggested a "rising authoritarianism" to come, Ceylon's democracy scores remained fairly high throughout this period (Barrow, 2014, 798). Bandaranaike was also able to thwart a coup conspiracy in 1962.

Over time, however, the government's socialist policies led to severe deficits and depleted the country's cash reserves (Abeynaike, 1963). The nationalization of private schools, insurance companies, and the oil industry brought criticism at home and abroad (Kodikara, 1973). As a result, the SLFP lost the 1965 elections. Out of office, Bandaranaike continued to lead the SLFP, stoking anti-Tamil sentiments among the Sinhalese population (Barrow, 2014).

4.2.2 The Autocratization Episode

The onset of the episode coincides with the May 1970 elections. The incumbent United National Party (UNP) failed to deliver economic progress over its five-year term and thus faced a resounding loss at the polls. Bandaranaike regained the top post, and over the next seven years, her government eroded democratic norms and went about implementing policies designed to replace the thriving and multi-ethnic democracy with a regime that was unapologetically exclusionary to ethnic and religious minorities (Barrow, 2014, 799).

In 1972, the government promulgated a new constitution that changed the country's name to the Republic of Sri Lanka (Government of Sri Lanka, 1972). It concentrated power in a unicameral parliament with supreme authority to make and repeal laws, undermining judicial autonomy. It also rescheduled elections from 1975 to 1977, extending Bandaraniake's term by two years. Buddhism was given "the foremost place," and Sinhalese was again recognized as the country's official language. This alienated the large Tamil population and other minorities in the country. It effectively meant the end of Ceylon as a secular state and the beginning of Sri Lanka as a Buddhist-Sinhalese-Socialist republic (De Silva, 2005).

Bandaranaike's second term stoked ethnonationalist sentiments while failing to address the country's economic situation. For the first time, schooling occurred in two separate languages, encouraging the Sinhalese and Tamil to grow and think as distinct communities. Changes introduced to university admissions strayed from the principles of merit and fairness and were designed to emphasize regional and ethnic identities (Wickramasinghe, 2012). The government also nationalized newspapers and the financial sector, imposed restrictions on land holdings, and reintroduced rice subsidies (Barrow, 2014). These policies, combined with high oil prices, led to rising costs of living and high unemployment rates (Barrow, 2014). As a result, Bandaranaike's popularity slipped.

Actions meant to favor the majority Sinhalese population destroyed relations with the Tamil minority group, who developed deep grievances over feelings that their rights could be arbitrarily taken away or circumscribed by the Sinhalese-dominated government without recourse to due process. This led to unrest and eventually the formation of the Liberation Tigers of Tamil Eelam (LTTE), an insurgent group agitating for an independent Tamil homeland in northern and eastern Sri Lanka (Bajoria, 2009). The Bandaranaike government responded by imposing a state of emergency across the island.

In July 1977, Sri Lanka held its first elections under the 1972 constitution. According to Bandaranaike, "I felt we would win. but in the last week, I knew that the trend was against us. By election night, I felt we would lose, but the size of our defeat surprised everyone. Even my opponents never expected it" (Buultjens, 1982, 15). The UNP won by a landslide, taking 140 out of 168 (83 percent) seats in the parliament. Meanwhile, the SLFP only won eight.

Afterward, Bandaranaike accepted defeat, arguing "I firmly believe in democracy" (Buultjens, 1982, 15).

Armed with a super-majority in an all-powerful parliament, Prime Minister J. R. Jayewardene now had virtually unchecked authority, which he used to wage an all-out assault on Sri Lanka's democratic institutions. A veteran politician from the independence struggle, Jayewardene rose through the ranks of the UNP, serving as a cabinet minister for fifteen years and the leader of the opposition throughout Bandaranaike's second term. Jayewardene admired "the developmental results achieved by his more authoritarian contemporaries elsewhere in Asia" and, thus, viewed electoral democracy as an impediment to economic progress (Venugopal, 2015, 676).

In particular, he sought to create a strong executive who could "stand above the petty bickering and fickle alliances of parliament" and make unpopular decisions free from the "the heat of electoral pressures" (Venugopal, 2015, 675–676). Shortly after taking office, Jayewardene introduced a constitutional amendment establishing a presidential system. The amendment redirected power from the prime minister to a president who acted as the head of government. The government did not allow public consultation on the issue, and the discussion in parliament included only six speeches before the amendment was adopted (Warnapala, 1979).

The following year, the parliament adopted a new constitution that consolidated power in an elected president and established a proportional representation system for legislative seats. The 1978 Constitution reinforced the ethnoreligious character of the state by including similar language concerning the preeminence of Buddhism but also tried to ease tensions by recognizing Tamil as a national language.

Afterward, Jayewardene narrowed the space for political opposition. Two laws adopted in 1978 provided the government sweeping powers to investigate and strip individuals of their political rights. Those subject to such "civic disabilities" could not defend themselves or appeal the decision (Warnapala, 1979, 182). In 1980, Jayewardene used these laws to disqualify Bandaranaike and her son from serving in public office for seven years.

Going one step further, Jayewardene enacted legislation that expanded the government's power to censor the press and gave the executive sweeping authority to intervene in political organizations, order detentions, and seize property. After enacting a ban on strikes for essential services, Jayewardene faced "remarkably few strikes" and easily crushed those that emerged, such as the railway strike in 1980 (Wriggins, 1981, 206). Restrictions imposed on local media houses led to self-censorship; meanwhile, foreign press faced expulsion or discrediting if it published articles critical of the regime (Bourne, 1983).

The judiciary was also not spared. Jayewardene introduced a constitutional amendment in 1983 requiring that all public servants make an "oath against separatism," which he then used to get rid of judges who opposed his rule (Bourne, 1983). According to one observer, "rules and regulations, formerly invoked in times of emergency, have now been made ordinary statute law" (Warnapala, 1979, 183)

In 1982, Jayewardene's government strategically decided to move up the date for elections, which were originally due for president in February 1984 and parliament in August 1983 (Samarasinghe, 1983). The government's market-oriented policies could not overcome the economic consequences of poor export earnings, declining tourism, and a severe drought. It faced increasing pressure from international financial institutions and foreign donors to implement structural adjustment programs. Thus, Jayewardene held elections early to avoid potential fallout from budget decisions in the coming year.

During the 1982 presidential campaign, Jayewardene promised to dissolve parliament immediately after being elected so that it could receive a fresh mandate. Given the overall climate of suppression, Jayewardene won with 53 percent of the vote. However, the results suggested that SLFP held large support at the grassroots and UNP would not be able to attain a sizeable majority under the proportional representation rules for parliament (Samarasinghe, 1983).

Now facing the loss of a super majority, Jayewardene instead called a referendum to extend the life of the parliament by six years. Jayewardene argued that the presidential poll had given the UNP a fresh mandate and that extending the life of parliament was also necessary for national security and development (Samarasinghe, 1983; Warnapala, 1983). He claimed that there was a conspiracy against his life amongst radical opposition elements; thus, holding parliamentary elections could possibly allow them access to the legislature (Bourne, 1983).

The referendum occurred nine weeks after the presidential election. During the campaign, several opposition members were in jail over the conspiracy, and a state of emergency was in place (Samarasinghe, 1983). As a result, the referendum passed with 55 percent of the vote. Afterward, the conspiracy against Jayewardene evaporated, with some suggesting that he had fabricated the plot (Bourne, 1983).

4.2.3 End of the Episode

According to the ERT data, Sri Lanka's democracy broke down after the events of 1982. Jayewardene went on to rule for another six years. During that time, Sri Lanka descended into political chaos and civil war.

In 1983, conflict broke out between the Tamil Tigers and the Sri Lankan military. The war lasted over three decades, making it one of the longest-running civil conflicts in Asia (Bajoria, 2009). India eventually sent a peacekeeping mission in 1987, but it failed to secure the separatist region, and they evacuated amidst escalating conflict three years later. This gave the Jayewardene government the pretext to further restrict the political space, circumscribe the powers of the judiciary, and censor the press and civil society, something his successor, Ranasinghe Premadasa continued but with less popularity (Freedom House, 1993).

Sri Lanka's democracy recovered after the 1994 election, when Chandrika Bandaranaike Kumaratunga, the SLFP candidate and Sirimoavo Bandaranaike's daughter, won the presidency with over 62 percent of the vote. Kumarantunga appointed Bandaranaike as Prime Minister, leading to her third term in the post. Since then, however, Sri Lanka's democracy has experienced ups and downs, largely due to persistent ethnic and religious tensions.

4.3 Conclusion

We can draw many parallels between the episodes in India and Sri Lanka. Both episodes begin under the leadership of the country's first woman prime minister. Sirimavo Bandaranaike and Indira Gandhi ascended to power following the death of their predecessors and were underestimated by their parties. They gained office largely because they were popular and because party leaders assumed they could be controlled. Each also held a reputation for being "soft-spoken" or "naive" (Buultjens, 1982; Encyclopaedia Britannica, 2020). Contrary to expectations, however, Gandhi and Bandaranaike quickly began to exert their independence and personalize their positions after taking office. They both gained and eventually lost popularity due to their socialist policies, which promised but ultimately failed to provide development and income equality to the masses. However, these two democracies met very different fates. While India's democracy managed to endure, Sri Lanka's descended into dictatorship and civil war.

Despite their similarities, we observe several key differences in how leaders in these two countries went about the executive aggrandizement process, and in particular, the nature of the populist rhetoric they employed. Whereas Bandaranaike chose to tap into the fractious ethnic divide in the country and weaponize the power of the Sinhalese majority, Gandhi was careful to avoid identity politics even though she could have weaponized her Hindu identity. In addition, while Gandhi employed legal instruments to undermine democracy – most notably the state of emergency clause in the constitution – she overestimated her popularity and underestimated the need to rely on institutions to cement her rule. By contrast, Bandaranaike's constitutional maneuvers inadvertently set the stage for the resurgence of UNP dominance and allowed Jayewardene to consolidate virtually unchecked executive authority.

Thus, while Gandhi and Bandaranaike made similar blunders that cost them their offices via elections, their actions while in power meant that their successors inherited very different institutional and societal conditions, which probably contributed to the divergent outcomes in these two cases. The nature of executive aggrandizement under India in the 1970s had less of a long-run impact on democratic institutions and norms when compared to Sri Lanka. And as a result, the former bounced back from this troubled period, while the latter ultimately failed. As we discuss in Section 5, however, India's democracy faced another grave threat that ultimately led to its failure in the twenty-first century.

5 Bulgaria and India

As illustrated in Figure 3, Bulgaria (2001–2018) and India (2000–2017) had similar levels of democracy when they experienced autocratization onset within one year of each other. Nevertheless, these cases exhibit several key differences. Bulgaria became a democracy only in 1990 after the collapse of communism, whereas India had been democratic since 1948. India's democracy had already proven itself resilient, having survived an earlier episode of democratic backsliding under Indira Gandhi in the 1970s (see Section 4). Thus, one might expect that being a less experienced democracy, Bulgaria had yet to fully entrench democratic norms within its society (Borissov, 2008), making it less resilient to incumbent-driven autocratization. Yet, according to the ERT data, the opposite outcome occurred. Democracy survived in Bulgaria, although it has yet to recover fully. Meanwhile, democracy broke down in India, and Prime Minister Narendra Modi continues to undermine democratic norms and institutions as of late 2022. What explains Bulgaria's democratic resilience and India's unexpected collapse?

5.1 Bulgaria (2001–2018)

5.1.1 Background: Leading up to the Episode

Amidst popular demands for reform, the ruling Bulgaria Communist Party (BCP) implemented a piecemeal reform process from above, resulting in the

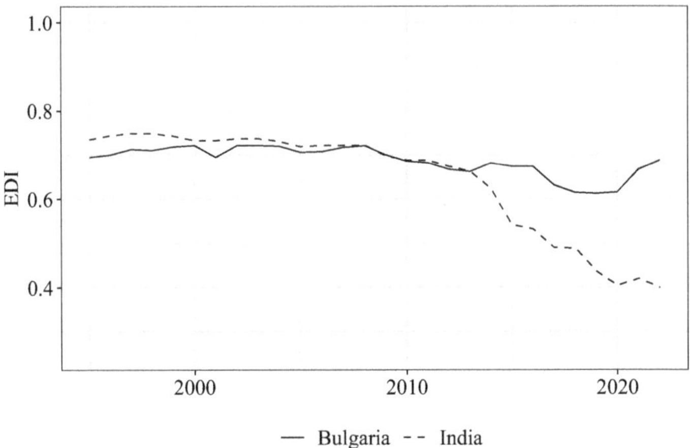

Figure 3 Electoral democracy in Bulgaria and India, 1995–2022

transition from a one-party communist regime to a multiparty democracy in 1990. Since then, the country has held regular competitive elections, with several turnovers in power and general respect for its people's political and civil rights.

Yet, several weaknesses in Bulgaria's budding democracy were apparent by the late 1990s. As a carryover from the communist era, journalists tended to view themselves as social and political leaders rather than mere informers, resulting in a "highly politicized and partisan" media landscape (Gross, 2002, 38). In addition, the judiciary remained weak and the least reformed branch of the government (Melone, 1996, 236). While the ruling party generally respected the courts' decisions, even when it had a large majority of the parliament (Drezov, 2000), budgetary constraints and uncertainty over the courts' composition and structure meant that there was "little reason to expect bold decisions" (Melone, 1996, 236).

Within this context, Bulgaria's last Tsar – Simeon Saxe-Coburg-Gotha II – reentered public life. Simeon II, who had been forced into exile as a nine-year-old following the communist abolition of the monarchy in 1946, spent much of his childhood in boarding schools in the United Kingdom and United States before settling in Spain. The New York Times later characterized him as "a man resigned to an outsider's role" (Whitney, 1997) and someone "anxious not to give offense" (Simmons, 1997). In 1996, Simeon II returned to Bulgaria to be greeted by crowds estimated to number a half million, larger than those who turned out in the successful pro-democracy protests in 1989 (Reuters, 1996). Yet polls showed that only about one-in-five Bulgarians supported restoring the monarchy (Reuters, 1996).

5.1.2 The Autocratization Episode

The episode began in 2001 with declines in freedom of association and expression. In February, the government appointed Ivan Borislavov as director general of the Bulgarian National Radio. Journalists protested his appointment as politically motivated. While the Bulgarian Supreme Court agreed and rescinded his appointment, the government dismissed journalists who had protested and replaced them with those loyal to the ruling party (Freedom House, 2002).

Later that year, the government replaced the National Council for Radio and Television, a regulatory body considered to be biased in favor of the government, with the Electronic Media Council. However, this council was also not free from possible political influence, being appointed by the president and parliament. The Bulgarian Helsinki Committee (BHC) at the time reported that many journalists felt constrained in their reporting due to government influence and also media management and outside pressures (State Department, 2002).

Meanwhile, in April 2001, Simeon II declared the formation of the Simeon II National Movement (NDSV) at his residence outside Sofia. The courts attempted to block the registration of the NDSV because their "papers were not in order" (CNN, 2002), and Simeon II was only able to register the NDSV after joining a coalition with the Party of Bulgarian Women and the Movement for National Revival (Freedom House, 2002).

Less than two months later, the NDSV secured exactly half the seats in the parliament, and Simeon II became the first deposed European monarch to hold a Prime Minister position (Chary, 2011). Amidst growing antiparty sentiment and declining trust in democratic institutions (Karatnycky et al., 2002), the NDSV gained support from virtually every corner of society, "regardless of income, age, or education and in 28 of the country's 31 regions" (Karatnycky et al., 2002, 128), without putting forward much by way of their policy proposals (Tagliabue, 2001).

The royal nostalgia that arose during the 2001 campaign led some to question whether Simeon II had plans to restore the monarchy. Instead, over the next five years, his party pursued a political agenda not all that different from his predecessor. According to V. I. Ganev (2006, 82), "It eschewed dramatic policy reversals and, overall, displayed a degree of concern for strengthening effective governance." As shown in Figure 3, the state of Bulgaria's democracy remained fairly consistent from 2001 to 2005, suggesting that not much backsliding occurred. The episode nearly ended there due to stasis.

The European Union (EU) accession process may have led to limited autocratization under the Simeon II government. After being left out in 1997 due to questions about its governance and economic reforms, Bulgaria was invited to talks in February 2000. Over the next several years, Bulgaria attempted to position itself as accession-worthy through piecemeal reforms in response to EU conditionalities. It had the benefit of comparison with Romania, another laggard much farther behind Bulgaria on reforms (Noutcheva & Bechev, 2008). After French and Dutch voters rejected the EU Constitutional Treaty in May 2005, Simeon II went to the polls for re-election under a cloud of uncertainty about Bulgaria's EU prospects, with accession plans facing potential delays.

The NDSV lost control of the parliament in the 2005 elections, but it served in a coalition government with the BSP until 2009. This discredited the party's claims to populism and monarchism given the baggage associated with the former communist party. Despite being characterized as an "almost forgotten episode" (Wien, 2021), the rise and fall of the Simeon II government had important consequences for Bulgaria's democracy going forward. It showed the extent of dissatisfaction with the prevailing political elite and the immense opportunities this situation posed for political entrepreneurs (Gurov & Zankina, 2013).

Out of these conditions arose a new personalist-populist party, the Citizens for European Development of Bulgaria (GERB). Founded in 2006 by Boyko Borisov, GERB has been characterized as having "no particular ideology" and "no coherent vision of Bulgaria's future" (V. I. Ganev, 2018, 96). Borisov's charisma is GERB's main resource, and he "leaves no doubt that he has full control of the party and the final say on all cabinet and party decisions" (Gurov & Zankina, 2013, 6).

Borisov spent most of the 1990s running a private security company before serving as a bodyguard and head of police for Simeon II. This experience allowed Borisov to successfully reinvent himself as a politician, winning the mayoral race in Sofia in 2006 (Smilov, 2008). Since then, Borisov has experienced a love-hate relationship with the Bulgarian people. Between 2009 and 2021, he served as prime minister three times, resigning twice due to protests in 2013 and the defeat of GERB's presidential candidate in 2017. Each time, Borisov returned to power. He did so by normalizing a personalist and highly corrupt regime and painting his critics as "hysterics with no feel for the realities of governing" (V. I. Ganev, 2018, 99).

As illustrated in Figure 3, Bulgaria experienced further erosion in democracy throughout the rest of the episode. Judicial independence and press freedoms suffered particularly large setbacks. This came despite Bulgaria's accession to the EU in January 2007 under unusual circumstances, which included continued monitoring of its judicial system (Noutcheva & Bechev, 2008). At the same time, the EU appears to have played a "passive" role during the episode. While the EU did withhold some funding from 2007 to 2009, the Borisov government experienced few repercussions for its failure to implement recommended reforms to the judiciary (Gherghina & Bankov, 2023). Rather, the opposite appears to have unfolded throughout the rest of the episode.

Under Borisov, executive aggrandizement primarily took the form of weakening and weaponizing judicial institutions. The judiciary became largely compliant with ongoing government corruption by subjecting proceedings to lengthy delays and dismissing charges on technicalities (G. Ganev et al., 2013). The non-transparent appointment procedures for judges and the non-random allocation of cases opened the courts to "political meddling" (Spirova, 2015). As V. I. Ganev (2018, 98) observes, "public figures who oppose[d] the government might run into legal trouble, and several former members of non-GERB cabinets have been placed under investigation"; however, this never rose to the level of "elaborately prepared abuses of judicial power." Still, the perception that the "[r]ule of law in many cases is only a fiction" drove down support for GERB and continued to erode public trust in elites and the democratic system (Krastev, 2016, 38).

The media environment also worsened with increased hate speech, violence against journalists, lack of transparency in media ownership and funding, and the "fusion of media and politics" (Zankina & Gurov, 2018). Between 2006 and 2018, Bulgaria dropped from 36th to 111th place on Reporters Without Borders press freedom rankings (Reporters Without Borders, 2023). Several independent print media outlets closed due to insolvency, and online sources with "questionable quality" rose in their place (Spirova, 2017). Meanwhile, journalists faced the threat of violence for speaking out against corruption and organized crime (Freedom House, 2011a). They were often pressured to support political actors (Spirova, 2017). The concentration of media into large monopolies owned by individuals with ties to Borisov and a lack of transparency over their ownership and funding sources reduced access to alternative sources of information (Zankina & Gurov, 2018).

5.1.3 The End of the Episode

By 2019, Bulgaria's democracy had reached its lowest point since the post-communist transition. Despite disapproval from the EU for its lack of reforms, Borisov's government faced few repercussions from the regional bloc. Fragmentation of the opposition also allowed Borisov to continue weakening

Bulgaria's democratic institutions without many consequences (Gherghina & Bankov, 2023). Nevertheless, the subtle erosion of democracy under the three GERB governments did not lead to a breakdown of democracy. Instead, a major blunder in mid-2020 eventually led to the conclusion of this episode.

In July 2020, a video on social media showed bodyguards from the National Protection Service stopping a center-right politician – Hristo Ivanov – from docking on a public beach. Later it came to light that the government had reserved the beach for Ahmed Drogan, a former politician, who had established a private port there for the summer (Barzachka & Yordanova, 2020). The video sparked outrage, and mass protests erupted. After the president criticized the incident, the prosecutor-in-chief raided his offices in retaliation (Dimitrova, 2022). This sparked further protests calling for the dissolution of the GERB government over the politicization of the Prosecutor in Chief's office, among other emerging scandals. Borisov refused to resign, and instead proposed a new constitution to placate the protestors' demands (Gherghina & Bankov, 2023). This strategy bought the government time while doing little to respond to the protests. Meanwhile, these events forced the fragmented opposition to form a *cordon sanitaire*, with the understanding that they would reject any agreement with GERB to a post-election coalition. This strategy effectively isolated GERB, leading to its loss of power in April 2021.

Since then, the political situation in Bulgaria has remained highly unstable (Yovcheva & Bértoa, 2023). There were five parliamentary elections between April 2021 and April 2023. As of this writing, Borisov has stepped back, refusing to take up a cabinet position or run for prime minister. However, GERB is a major partner in the coalition government formed in June 2023, and the prime minister position will rotate to Mariya Gabriel, a GERB member, in nine months (Camut, 2023).

5.2 India (2000–2017)

5.2.1 Background: Leading up to the Episode

Despite unfavorable conditions (Mainwaring & Masoud, 2022), India established the world's largest democracy immediately after independence. For the next fifty years, various factions of the centrist Indian National Congress party dominated politics. As discussed in Section 4, the 1970s saw a period of executive aggrandizement under Indira Gandhi that nearly destroyed India's democracy.

While democracy bounced back, the Emergency Period had a lasting impact on Indian politics. It saw the emergence of the first non-Congress government formed from a contradictory constellation of political parties unified solely in their opposition to Gandhi (Mendelsohn, 1978). Unsurprisingly the Janata government fell apart, but from its ashes arose the ethnonationalist Bharatiya Janata Party (BJP) (Gould, 1980).

The BJP is "a typical populist radical right party" (Leidig & Mudde, 2023, 360) that draws heavily upon Hindutva. Because Hindutva considers all "indigenous religions" as part of one Hindu nation, it is best described as an ethnonationalist ideology. To restore India to a mythical golden age, Hindutva claims that loyal Indians "should have superior rights and privileges; the less than fully loyal should have inferior rights, or maybe none at all" (Varshney, 2022, 108). It ascribes a superior place to Hindus, Buddhists, Sikhs, and Jains, who are "presumed to have natural fidelity to India, for their religions were born in India" (Varshney, 2022, 108). Through this distortion of history, Muslims and Christians are cast as foreigners and invaders with less loyalty and are, thus, less deserving of certain rights. With connections to fascist Italy and Nazi Germany, Hindutva first emerged in the colonial period. Early Hindutva thinkers argued that Hindus are the true Aryan race (Leidig, 2020; Thapar, 1996). Relegated to the fringes of political life throughout the first fifty years of Indian independence, Hindutva slowly gained prominence after the Emergency period.

Although the BJP performed poorly throughout the 1980s, it slowly developed a grassroots basis for support, eventually allowing it to gain power. A cadre-based system of local cells – or *morchas* – and training camps helped to "strengthen cadres' ideological commitments and organizational abilities" (Basu, 2012, 84). Capitalizing on growing discontent with Congress and its neoliberal economic reforms, the BJP took the most seats in the 1996 Lok Sabha elections (Pai, 1996). However, its fragile coalition government collapsed within 13 days, leading to a period of political instability and party realignment. The BJP again won the most seats in the Lok Sabha in 1998, but its government collapsed the following year, prompting fresh polls. Finally, with support for Congress at an all-time low, a BJP-led coalition was able to form a stable government in 1999.

5.2.2 The Autocratization Episode

The episode begins under the leadership of Prime Minister Atal Bihari Vajpayee, a veteran politician "virtually unknown outside India for most of his 50 years in politics" (McFadden, 2018). According to his obituary in the New York Times, Vajpayee was a moderate who supported equal rights for all religions, "championed women's rights and the eradication of castes," and "pushed back against militants in his own coalition" (McFadden, 2018). A careful reading of history contradicts this flattering portrayal. As a teenager, Vajpayee joined the Rashtriya Swayamsevak Sangh (RSS), a Hindu-nationalist paramilitary organization, before helping to form India's first Hindu nationalist party in 1951 – Jana Sangh – the predecessor of the BJP. During his term as prime minister, Vajpayee made subtle but fundamental shifts away from secularism, including mandated Hindu prayers in state-sponsored schools and revisions to history books to legitimate the Hindutva narrative (Freedom House, 2002; Ruparelia, 2006).

More disturbing, however, was the state-sanctioned political violence in Gujarat in March 2002 (Freedom House, 2003). After a railway fire in Gujarat killed sixty people, mostly Hindus returning from prayers, mobs swept through Muslim neighborhoods destroying property and killing thousands (Patil, 2017). Vajpayee refused to condemn the attacks and instead appealed to post-9/11 Islamophobia by suggesting that Muslims are inherently violent (Tully, 2002).

Seeking to capitalize on good economic conditions, Vajpayee called for early elections in 2004. The BJP had won several key state elections in late 2003, suggesting that it would easily secure a renewed mandate. In a surprising upset, however, the Congress-led United Progressive Alliance (UPA) coalition secured the most seats (Waldman, 2004). The UPA reversed many of the BJP's education policies. It emphasized the importance of the civil and property rights of all Indians, especially minorities (Freedom House, 2010) and sought to enact broad civic entitlements covering information, work, education, forest conservation, food, and even basic services (Nilsen, 2018; Ruparelia, 2013). However, the UPA's efforts to restore India's secular statism could not stem the growing popularity of the BJP's Hindu nationalist agenda, especially once it embraced a more hardline leadership under Narendra Modi in late 2013.

Described as a "first-rate orator with impeccable timing" (Waldman, 2002), Modi built a cult of personality for himself based on the "Gujarat model" of rapid economic growth and Hindu nationalism (Ding & Slater, 2021). Modi rose to the spotlight as the Chief Minister for Gujarat state, where he was complicit in the 2002 communal violence. He then capitalized on anti-Muslim sentiments to expand the BJP's majority in the state assembly through snap elections (Freedom House, 2003). Modi claimed credit for Gujarat's rapid economic growth, which outpaced other states. He promised to bring this "minimum government, maximum governance" model to the rest of India, giving him a strong following from the business and middle class, as well as youth and women (Mustafi, 2013; Waldman, 2002).[9]

---

[9] However, evidence suggests that Gujarat's economy was already booming, and Modi's policies had little effect on the state's economic trajectory other than exacerbating inequalities

Riding Modi's charisma, the BJP swept April/May 2014 national elections with 282 out of 545 seats (52 percent) – becoming the first ruling party since 1984 to win a majority of seats in the Lok Sabha (Inter-Parliamentary Union, 2014). Armed with a parliamentary majority, Modi almost immediately began undermining accountability mechanisms by consolidating powers within the executive. Within months of taking office, Modi had declared "all important policy issues" part of his portfolio and sidelined ministers by taking control of bureaucratic appointments (Daniel & Nair, 2015). In the Lok Sabha, the BJP sidelined the opposition by refusing to recognize the leader of the opposition and using a "guillotine" procedure to vote on legislation without debate (Khaitan, 2020, 67).

The courts, hitherto noted for their "judicial sovereignty" (Mehta, 2007, 70), showed "signs of subservience to the government" (Varshney, 2022, 116). After the courts blocked a constitutional amendment in 2015 that would have given the government more control over judicial appointments, senior BJP members publicly attacked the judiciary and the government delayed appointing judges. Since then, there have been several surprisingly favorable judgments for the Modi government, which analysts describe as motivated by ideological solidarity or self-preservation (Vaishnav, 2021).

The Modi government has systematically used security laws, criminal defamation, hate speech legislation, and contempt of court charges to silence critical voices (Freedom House, 2015; Ganguly, 2023). Indian journalists face intimidation and physical violence for running stories critical of the government (Gopalakrishnan, 2018). Twenty-two journalists were killed during Modi's first term, twice as many as under the previous government (UNESCO, 2023). Meanwhile, Modi's social media platform, launched in 2015, has amplified propaganda and disinformation by obliging members to follow BJP leaders (Ozturk, 2021).

In addition, Modi's government shut down critical civil society organizations, particularly those that promote minority rights. Between 2015 and 2022, seventeen thousand civil society organizations were denied registration or renewal (Varshney, 2022). When these tactics failed, the government targeted organizations with constant "surveillance, harassment, intimidation, imprisonment, injury, and death" (Tudor, 2023, 126). Meanwhile, groups promoting Hindu nationalism were supported and rewarded (Varshney, 2022). The Modi government has put to effective use the Unlawful Activities Prevention Act

---

through increased business-state ties and decreased public goods spending (Ghatak & Roy, 2014; Jaffrelot, 2015).

(UAPA), which saw a 72 percent increase in arrests, almost all of which deny the opportunity for bail (Tudor, 2023).

5.2.3 The End of the Episode

Drawing on direct appeals to Hindu nationalism, Modi's BJP has succeeded in dismantling the world's most populous democracy from within through a combination of legal and extralegal maneuvers. According to the ERT data, India ceased to be a democracy sometime in 2017. Since then, conditions have continued to erode under Modi's second administration.

In the April/May 2019 elections, the BJP secured even more seats (56 percent), and its coalition held a commanding majority (65 percent) of the Lok Sabha. Less than two months later, the government introduced amendments to the UAPA that provide greater powers to designate individuals as terrorists and jail them indefinitely without bail. These amendments went into law in August 2019, and since then, the Modi government has detained thousands of protesters and opposition figures (Schmall & Yasir, 2021).

In March 2023, Modi's greatest potential challenger, the grandson of Indira Gandhi – Rahul Gandhi, was sentenced to two years in prison for defamation, the minimum amount necessary to disqualify someone from holding public office. The Indian Supreme Court overturned the sentence but also seemed to side with the ruling party when it cautioned Gandhi "to be more careful as a public speaker" (Travelli, 2023).

Under Modi's second term, the government has become more open about its Hindutva vision for India. In August 2019, the government granted "an old Hindu-nationalist wish" when it revoked the autonomy of Jammu and Kashmir – India's only Muslim-majority state – placing it under direct rule from Delhi (Varshney, 2022, 110). Shortly thereafter, the Citizenship Amendment Act (CAA) came into law, providing a fast-track to citizenship for Hindus, Sikhs, Buddhists, Jains, Parsi, and Christians who illegally migrated to India from Pakistan, Afghanistan, and Bangladesh prior to 2015, thereby discriminating against Muslim migrants (Tudor, 2023). The government continues to revise the educational curriculum to remove or limit material about India's history and politics that is "inconvenient to its Hindu nationalist vision for the country" (Raj, 2023). The opening of the Hindu Ram Temple in Ayodhya, constructed where a Mosque stood for centuries before being destroyed by a mob in 1992, was strategically timed in early 2024 to coincide with the launch of Modi's reelection campaign. According to the New York Times, the event "was both a religious ritual and a made-for-TV spectacle for a broadcast media co-opted by Prime Minister Narendra Modi" (Mashal & Kumar, 2024).

5.3 Conclusion

Among the cases in this Element, Bulgaria's democratic backsliding is the least severe and most subtle. The uncertainty interval for the EDI overlaps at the beginning and end of the episode, suggesting the change was insignificant. Nevertheless, the decline is 15 percent, from 0.72 to 0.61. During his three terms, Borisov gradually undermined Bulgaria's democracy without fully incapacitating it. He acted as a personalist, strong-man leader while astutely avoiding inflammatory and divisive rhetoric that might attract ire from the EU. As V. I. Ganev (2018, 99) explains, "He does not try to play the role of an existential warrior engaged in epic battles with mighty enemies"; instead, "the source of Borisov's power is his ability to convince his fellow citizens that current Bulgarian political realities are not 'exceptional' but 'normal'."

Executive aggrandizement in Bulgaria involved the subtle erosion of media freedoms and judicial independence, two areas where democracy was already weak. In addition, the GERB government enabled an environment of rampant corruption; thus, much of the democratic backsliding in this case appears to be driven by desires for personal enrichment. This further eroded trust in democratic institutions and sent the country into an "electoral doom spiral" with five elections in twenty-four months (Yovcheva & Bértoa, 2023). Currently, various parties have struck an unlikely coalition that includes the GERB rotating into the premiership. Thus, while Bulgaria's democracy has survived for now, its resilience to future backsliding remains questionable.

The failure of India's democracy provides additional insights into democratic resilience. There is an argument to be made that all parties are guilty of undermining Indian secularism and democracy. Even before the current wave of Hindutva by the BJP, the Congress Party, in desperation, was already "jockeying for the support of different voting blocs and by stoking divisive issues of social identity (a practice known as vote banking)" (Jaffrelot, 2019, 2). The earlier episode (Section 4) of executive aggrandizement under Indira Gandhi also played an important role as a precursor to the current predicament by bringing Hindu nationalism into the majority coalition that eventually gave rise to the BJP. Gandhi and Modi engaged in similar tactics, including the repression of the media and civil society, the use of draconian laws to imprison political opponents, and the suppression of civil society.

Nevertheless, there are important differences between the two episodes. Gandhi ruled through personalist appeals, drawing on charisma and family legacy, but also strongly believed in a secular state and avoided exclusionary rhetoric. This makes her more similar to Bulgaria's leaders from 2001–2018. Simeon II built upon his family's royalty to briefly hold office, while Borisov appealed to machismo. Neither attempted to draw on xenophobia, unlike other nearby cases (e.g., Hungary in Section 7). By contrast, Modi and the BJP rely heavily on ethnonationalism. As Ganguly (2023, 145) explains, "Modi's drive to undermine democracy . . . is rooted in ideology. There is thus no reason to believe that the current antidemocratic onslaught will end." Indeed, the Indo-Aryan mythology underlying Hindutva also appears as a motivating force for Sinhalese nationalism in Sri Lanka. In both cases, colonial-era race theory enabled leaders to make similar appeals to the racial superiority of the majority ethnic group.

6 Ecuador and Turkey

Despite their geographic differences, Ecuador and Turkey shared many similarities at the start of the twenty-first century. Both countries experienced a democratic transition from military rule during the third wave of democratization. Incumbent elites initiated the democratization process in both cases, fitting the "reforma" model of regime change (Huntington, 1991; Linz, 1978). While Turkey's democratization was more protracted than Ecuador's, the two countries had achieved similar levels of democracy by the mid-2000s, as illustrated in Figure 4.

In both cases, autocratization occurred under the rule of a populist leader who came to power in the wake of political and economic instability. These autocratizing executives also deployed similar strategies to erode democratic institutions soon after taking office. Despite their similarities, the episodes ended with opposite outcomes. Democracy survived in Ecuador but collapsed

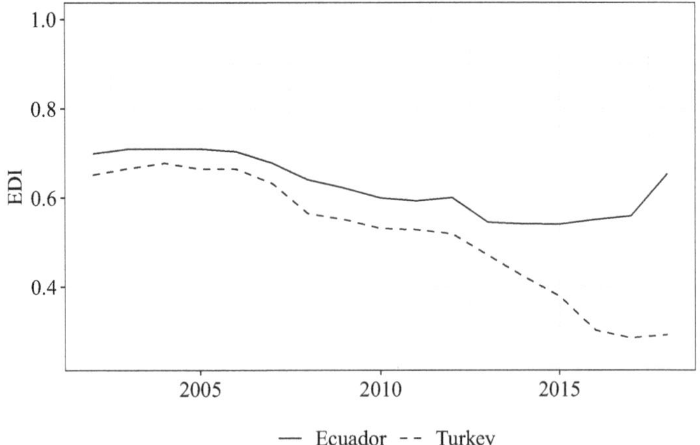

Figure 4 Electoral democracy in Ecuador and Turkey, 2002–2018

in Turkey. In the remainder of this section, we walk through each of these episodes to provide more context for how the process and outcomes differed between the two cases.

6.1 Ecuador (2007–2013)

6.1.1 Background: Leading up to the Episode

Ecuador experienced a major financial crisis and several changes in government in the decade leading up to the backsliding episode (Stoyan, 2020). Mass protests led to the pre-mature ouster of three presidents from 1997 to 2005, twice by legislative vote and once via a military coup. Citizens increasingly viewed traditional political parties as ineffective (Sanchez-Sibony, 2017). Public support for these parties "declined from an average of 70 percent between 1984 and 1998 to under 30 percent in 2006" (Haggard & Kaufman, 2021, 41). The low levels of confidence in the government and political system ahead of the 2006 presidential election created a beneficial environment for the anti-establishment and populist candidate Rafael Correa (Sanchez-Sibony, 2017).

Before running for president, Correa was an economics professor and briefly served as the Minister of Economy and Finance in 2005. Frequently described as a populist technocrat, Correa capitalized on the public's cynicism and launched a campaign centered around restructuring the entire economic and political order (De la Torre & Ortiz Lemos, 2016; Selçuk, 2016). Riding a left-turn in Latin American politics, Correa pledged to recenter the state's role in the economy to help it recover from the failures of neoliberalism (De la Torre, 2020). He also vowed to rewrite the constitution to "cleanse the body politic of its dysfunctional institutions" (Conaghan, 2008, 49). Correa's campaign proved successful; he won a runoff election in November 2006, becoming Ecuador's eighth president in a decade.

6.1.2 The Autocratization Episode

Almost immediately after taking office in 2007, Correa sought to remake Ecuador's political institutions. Following through on his campaign promise to replace the constitution, Correa issued an executive decree that mandated a referendum on establishing a constituent assembly. The decree created significant tension between the newly elected president and the Congress, as the latter believed Correa was overstepping his power (Conaghan, 2008). Despite winning the presidential run-off, Correa's party held no seats in the right-wing-controlled Congress.

However, Correa was able to move ahead with a nationwide vote in April 2007, and an overwhelming majority of the electorate supported creating a Constituent Assembly (De la Torre & Ortiz Lemos, 2016). Another national vote in September 2007 handed Correa's party 80 out of the 130 seats (62 percent) in the assembly, enough of a majority for his party to act without support from the opposition (Conaghan, 2008; Haggard & Kaufman, 2021).

Soon after its session started, the Constituent Assembly passed a mandate that substantially altered the distribution of power in the government. The mandate transferred all legislative authority from Congress to the assembly, forcing Congress into a temporary recess until the new constitution was finalized (Stoyan, 2020). This was a crucial move to help Correa solidify his influence over the new constitution and government during this period. Sidelining the right-wing controlled legislature removed a potential obstacle. Doing so through the popularly elected constituent assembly rather than by executive decree helped prevent pushback from below, especially since citizens were already dissatisfied with the existing Congress. This was all the more important given the recent history of Congress prematurely removing presidents from office.

Empowered by his majority in the Constituent Assembly, Correa oversaw the creation of a new constitution with a powerful executive branch. The document gives the president the power to dismiss Congress, hold national referendums, and veto or amend laws (Conaghan, 2016). It also allowed individuals to serve for two presidential terms, a change from the previous restriction barring consecutive terms in office. After the constitution was enacted, Correa called for new elections "as a symbolical move towards a brand new start for the country" (Selçuk, 2016, 581). The 2009 elections were a victory for Correa, and his party picked up a plurality of seats in Congress.

Beyond the constitutional changes, media freedoms were one of the primary victims of Correa's executive aggrandizement. The government confiscated radio and television stations, sued journalists for defamation, and pressured businesses not to advertise with opposition sources to economically weaken competitors (De la Torre & Ortiz Lemos, 2016). In 2009, the government passed a series of laws that regulated media reporting during election periods and put a moratorium on private media coverage of candidates forty-five days before an election (Cleary & Öztürk, 2022). Since the same restrictions did not apply to state-owned media outlets, the law allowed Correa to use government resources to build support for himself and his allies while reducing media coverage of opposition candidates in the immediate run-up to elections (Sanchez-Sibony, 2017). In 2013, Congress also passed a communication law establishing an agency responsible for regulating media content (Conaghan, 2016). This provided Correa another avenue through which he could monitor and silence media outlets that might be critical of his rule. Meanwhile, Correa frequently used the government television station to air mandatory national broadcasts highlighting the successes of his government while also discrediting his political and media adversaries (Selçuk, 2016). These broadcasts aired for nearly 12,000 minutes during his first five years in power (De la Torre & Ortiz Lemos, 2016).

Civil society also suffered throughout the episode. Correa required all organizations to register with the government and to abide by a series of vague rules that limited their operations (Goeury, 2021). His government used terrorism laws to restrict civil society organizations and to penalize individuals for engaging in protests (De la Torre, 2018). An executive decree issued in 2013 prohibited non-governmental organizations and movements from engaging in political activity or "interfering in public policies in a way that contravenes internal and external security or disturbs public peace" (De la Torre & Ortiz Lemos, 2016, 229). In addition to these coercive measures, Correa attempted to co-opt opposition groups by offering government jobs and other benefits (De la Torre & Ortiz Lemos, 2016; Laebens & Lührmann, 2021).

Finally, Correa's executive aggrandizement undermined the judiciary and the fairness of elections. A combination of laws, constitutional changes, and executive decrees allowed Correa to weaken and pack institutions like the judiciary with allies (Conaghan, 2016). Control over the courts helped insulate Correa from any legal challenges posed by political opponents (Cleary & Öztürk, 2022). Members of the National Electoral Council, the institution responsible for overseeing elections, were also loyal to Correa (Sanchez-Sibony, 2017). With the election-related media restrictions and bias of the National Electoral Council, the opposing presidential candidate in 2013 compared running in the election to "playing a soccer match on a tilted field and with a referee purchased by the other team" (De la Torre & Ortiz Lemos, 2016, 227).

6.1.3 End of the Episode

Throughout the episode, Correa relied on oil rents to fund his extensive social programs and patronage-based appointments (Mazzuca, 2013). However, when the commodity boom ended, and the price of oil dropped in 2015, Correa could no longer keep up with these high levels of spending. As a result, support for his government declined (Laebens & Lührmann, 2021; Sanchez-Sibony, 2017). Correa's popularity suffered further when he pressured Congress to remove presidential term limits to allow himself to run for a fourth term. Declining economic conditions, proposed tax increases, and growing frustrations with Correa's pursuit of another term sparked protests nationwide.

With his popularity sinking, Correa attempted to evade electoral defeat by setting up a caretaker government. He agreed not to run for the presidency and endorsed an ally, Lenín Moreno, as the ruling party's candidate (Cleary & Öztürk, 2022). With someone loyal in office, Correa could potentially still influence the government and return to power in 2021. However, this strategy proved to be a mistake.

After Moreno won the 2017 election, he worked to roll back the harmful reforms that took place under Correa's administration (Cleary & Öztürk, 2022; De la Torre, 2018) and pursued corruption charges against Correa and his associates (Laebens & Lührmann, 2021). Moreno actively worked to de-personalize politics, reinvigorated Ecuador's political institutions, and lifted restrictions on media and civil society (Stuenkel, 2019). Thus, although Ecuador's democracy appeared to be headed toward a breakdown, an economic downturn combined with Correa's miscalculations eventually allowed democracy to recover through a top-down process (Stuenkel, 2019).

Since then, things have not fared well for Correa, who has been living in exile in Belgium.[10] In 2018, he returned to Ecuador to campaign against the referendum restoring term limits. Far from a warm reception, "voters threw tomatoes and eggs at him on several occasions" and "he had to be evacuated by helicopter after rocks and trash were thrown at his car" (Ayala & Rochabrún, 2018). The result of the referendum effectively eliminated Correa's chances of returning to power, with 63 percent of voters supporting the restoration of term limits (IFES, 2018). In 2020, Ecuador's courts convicted Correa of accepting millions in bribes for public contracts, sentencing him to eight years in prison and banning him from political activities for 25 years (Cabrera, 2020).

6.2 Turkey (2005–2013)

6.2.1 Background: Leading up to the Episode

Turkey's protracted democratization throughout the 1980s and 1990s occurred under the watchful eye of its military with "a clear doctrine of modernization and a secularizing mission" (Yavuz, 2009, 31). By the early 2000s, Turkey was considered a model for democracy, secularism, and modernity in the Muslim world (Altunisik, 2005). However, it struggled to contain Islamist opposition.

---

[10] Belgium has denied extradition requests and granted Correa political asylum (Petrequin, 2022).

The courts engaged in a Sisyphean response to Islamist political activities, banning thirteen parties from 1991 to 1998. In the 1995 elections, the Islamist Welfare Party (RP) secured the most seats and led a brief coalition government from June 1996 until the military toppled it in a coup-by-memorandum in February 1997. The Constitutional Court banned the RP in 1998; it was promptly replaced by the Virtue Party, which the courts banned in mid-2001. This ban gave rise to the Justice and Development Party (AKP), founded by Recep Tayyip Erdoğan in August 2001.

The AKP's ideology is populist and ethnonationalist, with Muslimhood and Ottoman heritage as the core elements defining Turkishness, while also being moderate in its position concerning the West and capitalism by embracing neoliberal economics and making EU accession a high priority (Saraçoğlu & Demirkol, 2015). Erdoğan, an Islamist politician and the former mayor of Istanbul, had first joined politics in the 1970s as a youth winger for the Islamist National Salvation Party (MNP), the banned precursor to the RP. The closure of multiple Islamist parties made Erdoğan pragmatic in his approach to the APK. For example, after the RP was banned in 1998, Erdoğan told the New York Times, "If we want to attract more than 40 percent of the vote and come to power, we need a new image" (Kinzer, 1998). As a businessman, Erdoğan "hoped to reach beyond religious voters and appeal to the Turkish mainstream" by selling the AKP as a neoliberal Islamist party (Frantz, 2001).

The 2002 election saw a "collapse of centrist politics in the country" (Çarkoğlu, 2002, 30). Erdoğan's populism, combined with the AKP's promises to right the political and economic excesses of previous administrations, appealed to a wide cross-section of the population, including Islamists, rural nationalists but also the more moderate urban middle class angered by the previous government's economic policies (Cagaptay, 2002; Çınar, 2018; Dagi, 2008; Tepe, 2005; Yilmaz & Bashirov, 2018).

As a result, the AKP won a landslide victory, taking two-thirds of the seats in parliament. Only one other party – the left-leaning Republican People's Party (CHP) managed to secure seats (Cagaptay, 2002). However, Erdoğan was unable to serve in the parliament due to a 1998 conviction for "inciting hatred" (Lancaster, 2014; Tepe, 2005), a ban the courts upheld before the 2002 elections (Frantz, 2002). As a result, Abdullah Gül served as a caretaker prime minister for four months until the AKP government could repeal the ban and Erdoğan could secure a parliamentary seat through by-elections. This new position and the AKP's powerful majority set the stage for Erdoğan to dismantle Turkey's democracy from within.

6.2.2 The Autocratization Episode

Upon assuming office, the AKP government began implementing several "monumental reforms" in line with EU integration, including improvements to civilian oversight of the military, reduced restrictions on parties, and enhancements to the rule of law (Freedom House, 2005, 646). According to V-Dem, Turkey's electoral democracy index even improved from 0.65 to 0.68 during the first two years under the AKP, as illustrated in Figure 4.

The pace of reforms slowed in 2005 (Freedom House, 2006) when the backsliding episode began. Initial declines in democracy were subtle, largely due to a narrowing of space for the media and civil society. For example, in 2005, Erdoğan began to go after critics through defamation suits (Bermeo, 2016), and new legislation allowed the government to restrict activities of civil society groups (Freedom House, 2006; Gottlieb et al., 2023).

Backsliding intensified after the 2007 parliamentary election resulted in another victory for the AKP. This success allowed Erdoğan to retain his position as prime minister, and the AKP elected a new president aligned with the party (Szikra & Öktem, 2023). Despite the initial pushback from the opposition, the AKP successfully elected former prime minister and fellow party member Abdullah Gül as president (Çarkoğlu, 2007). With the parliament and presidency now controlled by his party, Erdoğan began to weaken other institutional constraints. The AKP government orchestrated a successful referendum in late 2007 to allow for direct presidential elections (Kalaycıoğlu, 2012), paving the way for Erdoğan to transform this largely ceremonial office into a strong presidency.

The judiciary became a primary target in 2008 after it ruled that the AKP's attempt to remove a ban on headscarves at universities was a violation of "the constitutional principle of secularism" (Cleary & Öztürk, 2022, 214), but unlike earlier courts, it stopped short of banning the AKP. In response, Erdoğan worked to curb the judiciary's power. In 2010, a set of constitutional amendments (by referendum) created judicial term limits, expanded the size of the Constitutional Court, and altered the process for appointing judges (Lancaster, 2014; Varol et al., 2017). These changes allowed Erdoğan to appoint individuals more favorable to his party, leading to a collapse of the separation of powers (Haggard & Kaufman, 2021).

The radically secular military continued to pose a major potential challenge for Erdoğan. In an effort to coup-proof the regime, the AKP made unsubstantiated charges that a secretive ultranationalist group known as Ergenekon was conspiring the topple the regime. Over several years, it used these claims to arrest an ever-widening number of individuals, including journalists and military officers. After securing another term in the 2011 elections, the government arrested a number of military officers leading to the resignation of the chief of staff and heads of the military branches. This gave Erodğan greater control over the selection of loyal commanders (Freedom House, 2012), helping to further insulate the AKP from pressure by secularist military officers.

Throughout the episode, attacks on the media and civil society amplified. Erdoğan and the AKP portrayed critical journalists as "enemies of the nation" and "outsiders of the Muslim community," evoking enthopopulism by calling into question their loyalty and Turkishness (Över, 2021, 347). The AKP has used this as justification to harass and arrest media opponents. Throughout the 2010s, Turkey regularly made the "worst offenders" list for jailed journalists (Getz, 2022). Critical media outlets also faced fines and property seizures, which often forced owners to sell to pro-AKP businessmen, who secured credit from state-owned banks (Över, 2021). While Turkey ranked 100 in 2002 on the World Press Freedom rankings, it had dropped to 154 by 2013 (Reporters Without Borders, 2023).

In 2013, Erdoğan's willingness to violently (and visibly) repress opposition to his regime dramatically escalated. After environmentalists gathered to peacefully protest the AKP's redevelopment of Gezi Park in May (Damar, 2016), police responded with excessive force (Sarfati, 2015). Outraged by this repression, demonstrations quickly spread throughout the country, with more than 3.5 million people participating at the height of the protests (Gençoğlu Onbaşi, 2016). Erdoğan's government violently suppressed the protesters, resulting in eleven deaths, over 8,000 injuries, and more than 5,500 arrests (Akyuz & Hess, 2018).

A few months after the Gezi Park incident, news broke of a corruption investigation involving several government elites and individuals connected to the AKP (Özbudun, 2014). Erdoğan claimed the accusations were a plot by the Gülen Movement, a rival to the AKP, to overthrow the government (Onbaşı, 2020; Taş, 2015). Afterward, he used the opportunity to purge several individuals suspected to be disloyal to his government from the police force, judiciary, and prosecutor's office (Akyuz & Hess, 2018; Freedom House, 2015) and limited internet access to tighten his control over the narrative (Çınar, 2018; Taş, 2015).

6.2.3 End of the Episode

According to the ERT dataset, Turkey's democracy broke down sometime in 2013, and its scores on the V-Dem EDI have continued to decline as illustrated in Figure 4. Turkey's EDI score fell from 0.68 in 2004 to 0.47 by the end of the episode, slipping further to 0.276 by the end of 2022. Even after the corruption scandal surfaced in late 2013, Erdoğan won the country's first-ever direct presidential election the following year. His success was partly due to his ability to rally support through populist and nationalist appeals, but he also benefited from an uneven electoral playing field (Freedom House, 2015; Türk, 2018). Observers cited irregularities during the election cycle and claimed that Erdoğan misused the media and other state resources to bolster his campaign (Freedom House, 2016).

In July 2016, a group within the military attempted to remove Erdoğan from office (Esen & Gumuscu, 2017). However, their efforts were unsuccessful, and Erdoğan used the failed coup as justification for further expanding his power. He declared a state of emergency in response to the event, which essentially enabled him to rule by decree until the order expired in July 2018 (Çınar, 2018). During this period, his government purged thousands of potential opponents from various state institutions and increased crackdowns on media freedom and civil liberties in the name of national security (Akyuz & Hess, 2018).

Erdoğan also used his new power to push through a referendum on a constitutional amendment that would transition the country to a presidential system. Although the state of emergency already "facilitated the switch to de facto presidential governance in Turkey," the constitutional amendment would officially move all executive power from the prime minister to the president (Akman & Akçalı, 2017, 579). The referendum passed in April 2017 and went into effect after the 2018 snap presidential elections (Freedom House, 2019). Erdoğan held on to power in the 2018 and 2023 elections, paving the way for him to continue leading the country further away from democracy.

6.3 Conclusion

Throughout most of the backsliding episode, Ecuador appeared to be headed down the same path as Turkey. Correa deployed several of the same tactics that Erdoğan used to consolidate power. Both executives altered their respective constitutions, appointed loyalists to key institutions, modified electoral laws, and curtailed media freedoms and civil society. Additionally, Correa and Erdoğan frequently used populist rhetoric and national referendums to bolster their legitimacy and support from the public. Despite these parallels, democracy remained resilient in Ecuador while it collapsed in Turkey. The two cases share many similarities in the nature of executive aggrandizement, including their emphasis on personalism, but the two executives diverged in their style of populism, which may have had important consequences for their legitimacy in times of crisis.

Correa embraced a technocratic style of populism, which inevitably meant that his popularity hinged upon positive economic performance. Throughout the episode, an oil boom fueled economic growth and investments in health and education, which helped reduce poverty and inequality (Stuenkel, 2019). This provided Correa with popular support, which he used to push through constitutional changes that eroded democracy by referendum. However, the economy experienced a crisis at a crucial time when Correa was also seeking to remove term limits. As a result, Correa was unable to contain rising opposition because he could not fall back on performance-based claims to legitimacy. There is also something to be said about the gross miscalculation Correa made toward the end of his rule. Unable to navigate mass protests and declining support for his regime, Correa chose the wrong successor for a would-be caretaker government, who not only prevented him from returning to office but also rolled back many of his authoritarian policies.

By contrast, Erdoğan draws upon ethnopopulist appeals to loyalty to derive popular support, which allows him to scapegoat and repress the opposition. The neoliberal orientation of the AKP also allowed Erogan to cultivate a reformist reputation during the early days of the regime. This strategy has (so far) been successful, with Erdoğan surviving an attempted coup, economic downturn, and corruption scandal. As a result, the once-model democracy for the Muslim world has been reduced to an authoritarian regime.[11]

7 South Korea, Slovenia, and Hungary

Our final set of cases – South Korea, Slovenia, and Hungary – shared several similarities at the start of their episodes. All three began backsliding after the mid-2000s. South Korea transitioned to democracy in 1988, with Hungary and Slovenia shortly thereafter in 1990. Thus, all three countries had been democratic for at least fifteen years prior to the episode. In all three cases, incumbents decided to implement democratic reforms in response to pressures from below (Bernhard, 1993; Bukowski, 1999; Koo, 2002). By the time the episodes began, levels of democracy were similarly high – with scores above 0.84 on the V-Dem EDI as shown in Figures 5 and 6.

Yet, while the quality of democracy suffered in all three cases, South Korea and Slovenia recovered before becoming autocratic. In these cases, democracy

---

[11] It is worth noting Turkey's EDI scores in 2022 were only slightly better than Morocco and worse than Algeria, Iraq, Kuwait, and Tunisia (Coppedge et al., 2023).

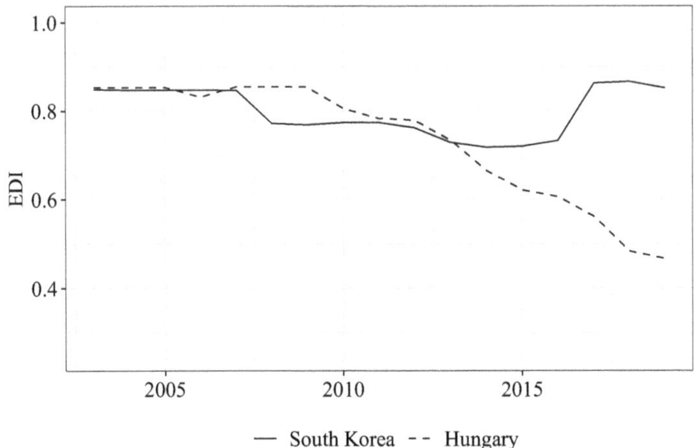

Figure 5 Electoral democracy in South Korea and Hungary, 2003–2019

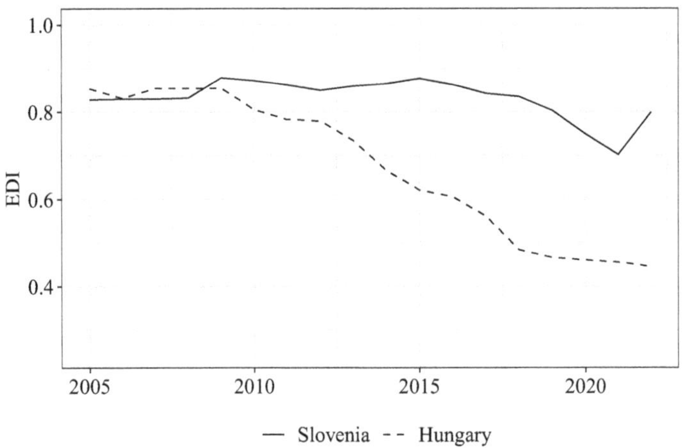

Figure 6 Electoral democracy in Slovenia and Hungary, 2005–2022

successfully rebounded when the autocratizing executive lost their hold on power after being impeached or voted out of office. Conversely, in Hungary, democracy broke down after enduring eight years of executive aggrandizement. We present narratives for each episode and then conclude with comparisons across the cases to shed light on why we might observe these diverging outcomes.

7.1 South Korea (2008–2014)

7.1.1 Background: Leading up to the Episode

After ruling for eight years as a military dictator, President Chun Doo-hwan agreed to allow direct presidential elections in 1987 amidst widespread student protests (Koo, 2002). Afterward, South Korea transitioned to democracy, but the authoritarian successor party remained in power until the liberal opposition won elections in 1997. The political situation grew increasingly turbulent during Roh Moo-hyun's presidency. In 2003, allegations surfaced of a corruption scandal involving several government elites and legislators "from across the political spectrum," including some individuals connected to Roh (Freedom House, 2008, 652). Less than a year later, the opposition-led parliament voted to impeach Roh for violating an electoral rule. While the Constitutional Court reinstated him (Brooke, 2004), popular support for the ruling party declined throughout the rest of his term (Chaibong, 2008).

These events set the stage for conservative candidate, Lee Myung-bak, to win the presidency in December 2007. Born to a poor family, Lee spent most of his career as the CEO of Hyundai, earning the nickname bulldozer for his get-the-job-done leadership style (Sang-Hun, 2007). Throughout the campaign, Lee promised to implement "populist reforms that would lead to a return to the kind of high economic growth seen previously during the ... dictatorship era and connected this to ultra-conservative condemnation of the legacy of 'leftist' presidents" (Doucette, 2010, 23). Once in office, President Lee began eroding democratic institutions. This backsliding occurred throughout his term and continued under his successor Park Geun-hye, the daughter of former dictator Park Chung-hee.

7.1.2 The Autocratization Episode

The episode begins in 2008, the first year of Lee's administration. In April, conservative parties won an "overwhelming majority" of seats in the legislature (Chaibong, 2008, 128). Shortly thereafter, Lee sought to improve economic relations with the United States by allowing beef imports, banned since 2003 due to concerns about mad cow disease (Choi, 2022). Hundreds of thousands of protestors took to the streets of Seoul in mass demonstrations that lasted for over forty days, evolving from the narrow issue of beef imports to include a range of issues such as healthcare, consumer prices, and education. In response, South Korean police raided offices of protest groups, arresting several dozen (New York Times, 2008b). The government also pressed charges against investigative journalists who had published a television program that sparked the protests (Choi, 2022).

Lee's attacks on media freedom and civil liberties were not isolated to the 2008 protests. Throughout his time in office, he relied heavily on defamation laws – which are a criminal offense – to silence and intimidate individuals and journalists who were critical of his administration (Haggard & You, 2015).

Lee also filled senior management positions at media companies with his allies and censored online comments (Gottlieb et al., 2023). As a result, Freedom House reclassified South Korea from "free" to "partly free" in its annual freedom of the press survey in 2011 (Freedom House, 2011b).

Lee also turned to the National Security Law (NSL) to penalize his critics (Gottlieb et al., 2023). The 1948 law was originally presented as a safeguard against North Korea and the spread of communism, but government elites often used the law to punish political opposition. While Lee was not the first South Korean leader to abuse the NSL, the number of arrests under his administration increased substantially compared to those that occurred under the two previous presidents, Kim Dae-jung and Roh Moo-hyun (Amnesty International, 2012; Haggard & You, 2015). Democracy further suffered due to the government's involvement in illegally surveilling citizens in 2010 (Croissant, 2019; Laebens & Lührmann, 2021).

The South Korean constitution limits presidents to one five-year term, so Lee could not run for the presidency again in 2012. However, the backsliding episode continued. Rocked by corruption scandals, Lee's approval ratings stood at around 20 percent, and there was an overall "gloomy outlook for the governing Grand National Party" due to dissatisfaction over the economy amidst the global recession (Sohn & Kang, 2013, 199). Yet conservatives were able to pull off a stunning victory in the parliamentary and presidential elections in 2012 under the leadership of Park Geun-hye, daughter of the former dictator Park Chung-hee.

Described as "a small woman of regal bearing" (Fackler, 2012), Park experienced twin tragedies, with her parents being assassinated five years apart. Later, she joined politics as a member of parliament and rose through the ranks of the GNP. During the 2012 campaign, Park drew on nostalgia for her father's "fabled high-growth era" to rebrand and reshape the GNP in her own image as the Saenuri Party (Doucette, 2010, 851). She attracted throngs of excited conservative supporters like a "movie celebrity, or even a religious figure" (Fackler, 2012). With promises of welfare and "economic democratization," Park was able to successfully distance herself and the party from Lee's excesses, reframing the campaign discourse from a retrospective to a prospective election (Sohn & Kang, 2013, 200).

During the 2012 campaign, Park's party also secretly worked with state security agencies to tilt the playing field. National Intelligence Service (NIS) operatives established thirty teams of experts on psychological warfare who sent over 1.2 million tweets praising Park and criticizing the opposition in an effort to help her get elected (Freedom House, 2014). According to a later NIS report, "The teams were charged with spreading pro-government opinions and suppressing anti-government views, branding them as attempts by pro-North Korean forces to disrupt state affairs"(McCurry, 2017). Security services also reportedly leaked transcripts from a meeting between former liberal President Roh Moo-hyun and North Korean President Kim Jong Il in an effort to stoke anti-leftist sentiments (Doucette, 2010).

Although she publicly apologized for her father's brutal dictatorship, Park's behavior in office was "not unfamiliar to citizens who experienced her father's draconian rule" (Croissant, 2019, 17). Park's leadership style was highly personalist and uncompromising. She expected "all within government to follow her lead without questioning" and labeled anyone who expressed a different view as disloyal (Hahm & Heo, 2018, 650). Despite campaigning on a reformist agenda, Park filled positions with hardline conservatives whose "style of politics reminded many of the dictatorship era" (Doucette, 2010, 854). Cronyism was a pressing issue as Park filled several ministerial positions with close personal allies, a practice that often resulted in scandals for her administration (Hahm & Heo, 2018).

Park continued the trend of curtailing civil liberties and repressing the media. During Lee's four-year administration, South Korea's World Press Freedom ranking slipped from 39 to 44. Within the first two years of Park's rule, it plummeted to 57 (Reporters Without Borders, 2023). Censorship became more intense after the 2014 Sewol Ferry disaster. Under Park's administration, the Ministry of Maritime Affairs and Fisheries improperly licensed the Sewel Ferry, which sank in 2014 killing 304 passengers (Gottlieb et al., 2023). Citizens protested the government's mishandling of the situation and Park's slow public response in addressing the crisis (Hahm & Heo, 2018). Park's administration responded with increased repression. Citing concerns about political rumors, Park had the prosecutor's office establish an antidefamation cyberinvestigation team that censored social media and text messaging. As a result, seven out of ten South Koreans reported being concerned about government surveillance of their online activities (Freedom House, 2015).

7.1.3 End of the Episode

While Park managed to remain in office after the Sewol ferry disaster, another major scandal ultimately ended her presidency and the backsliding episode. In October 2016, news broke that Park's longtime advisor Choi Soon-sil had access to confidential government information, influenced political decisions, and extorted $65 million from over fifty companies by threatening government retaliation (Freedom House, 2017; Sang-Hun, 2016). Mass protests erupted nationwide calling for Park's resignation. Investigators later ruled that Park was a criminal accomplice in Choi's influence-peddling schemes (Sang-Hun, 2016). This prompted the National Assembly to impeach Park in December 2016, and the Constitutional Court formally removed her from office in March 2017 (Sang-Hun, 2017). Park was sentenced to twenty years for bribery and other crimes but received a pardon in 2021 after serving four years of the sentence.

Park's impeachment in 2016 allowed democracy to recover and remain resilient, thus cementing 2014 as the end of the backsliding episode since the EDI did not decline further between those two years. Since then, South Korea's democracy has reequilibrated (Linz, 1978) back to levels slightly higher than before the episode.

7.2 Slovenia (2011–2021)

7.2.1 Background: Leading up to the Episode

Slovenia was the first among the Yugoslav republics to begin the political liberalization process after pro-reformists gained power in the late 1980s. By the time it declared independence in 1991, Slovenia had ousted the former Communist party through free and fair elections and had adopted a new democratic constitution. As a result, Slovenia became known as "a quiet success story, standing out against the tumult and destruction that marks its Yugoslav neighbor" (Hottelet, 2001). However, given its good relations with the West and the fact that the economy had done well under communism, Slovenia was also "a reluctant reformer, doing very little to actually change its institutional setup from the communist past," which left the country in a state of "unfinished democratization" (Bugaric & Kuhelj, 2015, 274).

Prior to the backsliding episode, Slovenia was hit particularly hard by the 2008 global financial crises (Krašovec & Lajh, 2021). Its GDP fell by 8.1 percent in 2009 and unemployment hit 7.8 percent by December 2010 (Guardiancich, 2012). The ruling coalition, led by Prime Minister Borut Pahor's Social Democrats (SD), pursued reforms to reduce the debt through austerity measures that decreased spending on social benefits (Freedom House, 2012). Voters rejected these unpopular reforms through a referendum in June 2011. The political situation became increasingly unstable throughout the year as the ruling coalition fell apart and the economy continued to decline. By the end of the year, the president was forced to call for early elections, which resulted in a center-right coalition government headed by Janez Janša's Slovenian Democratic Party (SDS).

A far-right populist who is often compared to Viktor Orbán and Donald Trump, Janša "applies a strange mixture of populism, egalitarianism, xenophobia, anti-intellectualism, and intolerance toward marginal groups with a political discourse and iconography which reminds one at the same time of Naziism and Stalinism" (Rizman, 1999, 159). Janša began his political career in the communist youth wing before defecting to pro-democracy movement in the 1980s – during which he was imprisoned for eighteen months. As Slovenia's first postcommunist Minister of Defense, Janša was accused of illegally smuggling weapons to Bosnia and refused to prosecute military police who beat up a civilian (Bilefsky, 2008; Marquand & Bowers, 1994).

Before his party's success in the 2011 elections, Janša had served as prime minister from 2004 to 2008. His first term contributed greatly to the polarization of Slovenian politics, as his government used its small majority to push through policies without compromise (Krašovec & Johannsen, 2016). According to Freedom House, journalists also experienced "indirect political and economic pressure" from government officials who treated them "like political opposition" during Janša's first administration (Freedom House, 2007b, 273). Support for the SDS fell after allegations surfaced about Janša's involvement in a major bribery scandal with the Finnish defense company Patria (New York Times, 2008a). However, Janša remained in parliament, ready to return to power once his party won the 2011 election.

7.2.2 The Autocratization Episode

After resuming his role as prime minister in January 2012, Janša quickly began targeting media freedoms. His government repressed critical journalists and expanded its influence over the public media outlet, RTV Slovenia, by ousting members of the supervisory board who were appointed by the previous center-left government (Freedom House, 2013; Milacic, 2022). However, Janša was unable to significantly weaken other institutions during his second term as prime minister.

After only a year, the SDS coalition fell to a vote of no-confidence amid unpopular economic reforms and continued concerns about government corruption (Freedom House, 2014; Krašovec & Johannsen, 2016). Four months later, Janša was found guilty in the Patria bribery case that came to light in 2008. He was sentenced to serve two years in prison, but the Constitutional Court overturned his conviction and the case expired before being retried (Freedom House, 2016).

Slovenia's electoral democracy score improved slightly over the next few years, but not enough to officially bring the backsliding episode to an end. Political polarization intensified, and corruption concerns plagued both the center-left ruling coalitions and opposition parties over the next three parliamentary cycles (Lovec, 2017, 2018). The coalition led by Prime Minister

Alenka Bratušek that took power in February 2013 collapsed by the summer of 2014. It was replaced by a new coalition headed by the Prime Minister Miro Cerar. Cerar's government ended early in 2018 when the Constitutional Court annulled a railway referendum ruling because the government's use of funds during the campaign may have unfairly influenced the result, prompting Cerar's resignation (Anderson, 2018). Thereafter, a minority center-left coalition was formed but fell apart in early 2020.

The most substantial decline in Slovenia's EDI occurred after Janša became prime minister for a third time in March 2020. As before, Janša's SDS-led government targeted media freedoms by verbally attacking and intimidating journalists, changing the leadership of the national media supervisory board, and withholding funding from critical sources while extending additional funding to media allies (Freedom House, 2022; Novak & Lajh, 2023). Janša also attempted to alter the legal frameworks governing freedom of speech by introducing legislation that would increase government influence over public media, while reducing its funding (Freedom House, 2021).

The COVID-19 pandemic provided Janša with greater cover for engaging in executive aggrandizement. His government used the Communicable Diseases Act to crack down on anti-government protests and nongovernmental organizations (Lovec, 2021). The Constitutional Court attempted to curb the government's abuse by declaring some provisions unconstitutional, but Parliament amended the law to allow the government to continue passing certain restrictions by decree (Freedom House, 2022). After the first wave of COVID-19 swept through the country, allegations arose that several government officials were involved in a scandal concerning the procurement of personal protective equipment and ventilators (Krašovec & Lajh, 2021). However, Janša's government had weakened the country's anticorruption institutions by not appointing public prosecutors to handle the corruption allegations (Freedom House, 2022).

7.2.3 End of the Episode

During his third term as Prime Minister, Janša's ability to make radical institutional changes to Slovenia's democracy was severely hampered by the bi-partisan nature of his government, which included center-left parties. Somehow, Janša managed to hold this fragile coalition together until regularly scheduled elections. The backsliding episode ended with the SDS defeat to a center-left coalition in the April 2022 poll.

Janša's abuse of power, coupled with his government's mishandling of the COVID-19 crisis, cost his party crucial support at the ballot box. While Janša had taken several steps to erode Slovenia's democracy, electoral accountability prevented him from permanently damaging it (at least for now). The current coalition government led by Prime Minister Robert Golob and the Freedom Movement (GS) party has taken steps to depoliticize the public media through an independent oversight board (Freedom House, 2023). However, given Janša's phoenix-like quality for returning to power, the future of Slovenia's democracy remains uncertain.

7.3 Hungary (2006–2018)

7.3.1 Background: Leading up to the Episode

Like Slovenia and South Korea, Hungary's most recent transition to democracy was an elite-driven affair (Rizman, 2006). Facing an economic downturn, pro-reformists took control of Hungary's Communist party in the mid-1980s and then strategically encouraged the growth of civil society so that they could stage roundtable talks leading to the democratic transition (Bernhard, 1993). Thus, Hungarian Communists negotiated democracy from a position of strength (Renwick, 2006) and likely sought to prolong their rule through new legitimation strategies (Slater & Wong, 2013). While the Communist successor party – the Hungarian Socialist Party (MSzP) – was roundly defeated by the center-right in the 1990 elections (Racz, 1991), it returned to power in a landslide victory four years later.

The 1994 election was a turning point for Hungary's fragmented political right, which subsequently experienced "progressive electoral and organizational concentration in a single party, Fidesz" (Fowler, 2004, 80). Founded as a pro-democracy liberal youth organization in the waning days of Communism, Fidesz performed miserably in the second post-communist elections. Afterward, under the pragmatic leadership of Viktor Orbán, Fidesz remade itself as a socially conservative populist party. This paid off in 1998, with Fidesz winning the most seats in the parliamentary elections. Early on, commentators expressed concerns about Orbán's "alarmingly nationalist statements" (Rosenberg, 1998). Once in office, Orbán centralized authority in the executive and reduced oversight of the parliament (Racz, 2003); however, these maneuvers did not seriously undermine democracy, at least according to Hungary's EDI scores.

Fidesz lost power to the MSzP in 2002 in a narrow election. The left-wing coalition won again in 2006, making it the first incumbent government to be re-elected since the fall of communism. These two electoral defeats further radicalized Fidesz, which began a "transformation from conservativism to illiberalism" (Bernhard, 2021, 596).

7.3.2 The Autocratization Episode

The episode began in the aftermath of the 2006 parliamentary election. Leaked recordings from an MSzP meeting revealed that Prime Minister Ferenc Gyurcsány had lied about the country's economic performance to boost his party's electoral chances (Freedom House, 2007a). Fidesz, still angry about losing the election, capitalized on the public's disapproval and stoked violent protests demanding Gyurcsány's resignation (Dempsey, 2006; Oltay, 2006). Over the next four years, the situation remained fairly stable, without enough improvement to end the episode. However, the fallout from the scandal and the worsening economic situation during the global financial crisis discredited the ruling MSzP coalition.

Fidesz swept the 2010 election by a landslide (Freedom House, 2011a), at which point democratic backsliding intensified considerably. Orbán used his party's super-majority to unleash a "legislative storm" on Hungary's democratic institutions (Rupnik, 2012; Szikra, 2014). The Fidesz government adopted over a dozen constitutional amendments and hundreds of laws in 2010 and 2011, which "profoundly affected the very foundations of the rule of law" (Bankuti et al., 2012; Rupnik, 2012).

One of these amendments reduced the voting requirements for creating a new constitution, which enabled Fidesz to engage in a "constitutional revolution" (Jenne & Mudde, 2012). In 2011, Fidesz hastily adopted a new Fundamental Law of Hungary without public debate or support from other parties. The new constitution substantially weakened the ability of the judiciary and parliament to check executive authority (Bankuti et al., 2012). The document is "imbued with national and social conservatism" (Pirro & Stanley, 2022, 92), including "cardinal laws" on culture, religion, and morality that require a two-thirds majority to change (Freedom House, 2012).

To ensure the judiciary would not reverse these legal maneuvers, Orbán's government packed the courts with loyalists through twin strategies of replacement and expansion (Kosař & Šipulová, 2023). The new constitution reduced the mandatory retirement age of judges from 70 to 62 years, forcing 274 judges out of office in early 2012 (Halmai, 2017) and increased the size of the Constitutional Court from 11 to 15 members (Rupnik, 2022). These vacancies opened the door for the Fidesz to pack the judiciary with individuals aligned with the party. While a European Court of Justice (ECJ) ruling eventually reversed the reduced retirement age, the damage was already done. Orbán's government provided financial compensation and reappointed the judges in different positions (Halmai, 2017). When the Hungarian courts tried to push back against

Orbán's overreach, his party amended the constitution in 2013 to further curtail the courts' powers (Kelemen, 2017, 223).

Orbán's government also made changes to the electoral framework to maximize Fidesz's success in future elections. These changes included eliminating 187 parliament seats, redrawing constituency borders, and increasing the percentage of votes needed to win a seat in the parliament (Freedom House, 2012; Gottlieb et al., 2023). Fidesz undermined the independence of the Electoral Commission by packing it with loyalists (Bankuti et al., 2012). Changes to campaign and advertisement rules before the 2014 elections also gave Fidesz "an undue advantage … that blurred the separation between political party and the State" (OSCE, 2014, 1). By extending voting rights to ethnic Hungarians living abroad, Fidesz has also been able to capitalize on Orbán's popularity among the diaspora (Gottlieb et al., 2023; Haggard & Kaufman, 2021). These changes have tilted the playing field, making it easier for Fidesz to maintain its super-majority in parliament.

Beyond constitutional and electoral changes, Orbán also worked to weaken other accountability institutions and actors that could threaten his power. To extend his control over the media, Orbán routinely repressed journalists and media outlets that criticized his government (Freedom House, 2022; Scheppele, 2022). In 2011, the Fidesz government required all media outlets to register with the newly established National Media and Infocommunications Authority (Rupnik, 2022). Media outlets that failed to register or aired content violating the government's rules could be fined or shut down (Freedom House, 2016). This enabled the government to monitor and restrict critical media sources more easily. Fidesz has also successfully "colonized" the state media allowing it to reach its supporters more easily, outsource programming and advertising to companies owned by its supporters, use state media jobs as patronage, and deny access to rival parties (Bajomi-Lázár, 2013). Orbán also has indirect influence over the private media through "government-friendly cronies" who own several of the major outlets in the country (Gottlieb et al., 2023; Rupnik, 2022). As a result, Hungary dropped from 23 to 73 on the World Press Freedom Index between 2010 and 2018 (Reporters Without Borders, 2023).

7.3.3 End of the Episode

According to the ERT dataset, Hungary's democracy broke down in 2018. For the second straight election, international monitors concluded that Fidesz benefited unfairly from official state resources, adding that "intimidating and xenophobic rhetoric, media bias and opaque campaign financing constricted the space for genuine political debate, hindering voters' ability to make a fully-informed choice" (OSCE, 2018, 1). Fidesz secured a third super-majority mandate, which it has extended further in the most recent 2022 elections. As of this writing, Orbán and Fidesz remain in power and autocratization continues.

7.4 Conclusion

While South Korea, Slovenia, and Hungary show several similarities, we observe important differences in the nature of executive aggrandizement. In South Korea and Slovenia, leaders predominantly focused on eroding media freedoms and civil liberties but left the institutional framework largely intact. By contrast, in Hungary, a legislative supermajority and early court packing produced a "collapse of the separation of powers" (Haggard & Kaufman, 2021), which enabled Orbán to engage in an "autocratic legalism" that effectively usurped accountability (Scheppele, 2018). Thus, Orbán consolidated power with less resistance than leaders in South Korea and Slovenia.

Orbán was also more successful at maintaining public support through charisma and nationalist rhetoric that stokes xenophobic fears of migrants and the dilution of Hungarian culture (Maerz & Schneider, 2020). For example, Orbán has urged against relationships with non-Europeans to avoid becoming a "mixed-race," arguing this results in "nothing more than a conglomeration of peoples" with no nation (Gijs & Fota, 2022). Orbán has also largely managed to avoid any major scandals that would prompt significant push back and now enjoys a heavily tilted electoral playing field and packed justice system. All of this makes it increasingly difficult to dislodge Fidesz from power and has allowed it to transform Hungary into an electoral autocracy.

Presidents Lee and Park of South Korea, on the other hand, did not engage in radically divisive rhetoric and instead relied upon more traditional conservative populism. Both leaders also only held a slim majority of seats in the parliament, making it difficult for them to pursue any major institutional changes without opposition support. As such, while these two leaders undermined media freedoms and attacked civil liberties, they largely did so within existing legal frameworks and under the constraints of watchful courts. Park's corruption left her unable to rally enough support to remain in office. After the 2016 Park-Choi scandal, several members of her own party even turned against her and voted in favor of her impeachment (J.- M. Park & Kim, 2016). With judicial independence intact, Park's impeachment and corruption trial went forward, ultimately leading to democratic resilience.

By contrast, Slovenia initially appeared to be headed down a path similar to Hungary. Like Orbán, Janša became increasingly more radicalized and populist after his first stint as prime minister. He also accelerated and intensified his attacks on democracy each time he returned to power. However, his party never enjoyed a majority in parliament and could not rely upon coalition partners to effect significant institutional changes. Further, like Park, Janša found himself at the center of several corruption scandals that eroded his popularity among voters and other parties in the parliament. Without strong support in these areas, Janša struggled to amass power and control accountability institutions as effectively as Orbán in Hungary. Though democracy appears to be recovering under a new government, we are cautious about Slovenia's resilience due to how recently the episode ended. The SDS still holds some seats in the parliament, and Janša remains eligible to serve again as the prime minister in the future. His return to power could be challenging to democracy given his previous attempts at executive aggrandizement and his close connections to Orbán in Hungary (Krekó & Enyedi, 2018).

8 Discussion and Implications

Writing about the Emergency period in India, Henderson (1979, 947) notes, "Democracies are perhaps threatened less by those who unashamedly put forward dictatorship than by those who have a hankering for that road but pose as democrats." In recent years, incumbent-led autocratization appears to be on the rise. Executives engage in deliberate and often legal tactics to undermine institutions of accountability and erode democracy from within. This phenomenon of executive aggrandizement contrasts with more abrupt seizures of power through military coups, autogolpes, and pigeon-hole constitutions observed during the previous wave of autocratization in the 1960s to 1970s. Understanding the process and how democracies can remain resilient is a central concern for scholars and policymakers.

According to Bermeo (2022), "the comparative study of how individual countries resist or reverse backsliding is essential." This Element has investigated nine cases where democratically elected governments engaged in executive aggrandizement that posed a real threat to democracy. Through structured focused comparisons of similar cases with different outcomes (Eckstein, 1975; George & Bennett, 2005), we uncover recurrent patterns in the process of executive aggrandizement. We also identify several factors that might help to explain why some democracies survive. In this final section, we synthesize the main conclusions and offer suggestions for future research.

8.1 Patterns of Executive Aggrandizement

The process of executive aggrandizement across all nine cases exhibited similar patterns. Most notably, the autocratizing executives in our cases often targeted the same actors – including media, civil society, and the judiciary – and used similar tactics to erode democracy – including installing loyalists, engaging in cooptation through state resources, and amending or changing legal frameworks. This suggests that incumbents pursue a fairly common playbook when dismantling democracy from within (also see Sato et al., 2022).

Diagonal accountability institutions, like the media and civil society, were among the most common targets. Media freedoms suffered due to a combination of direct and indirect government attacks. In Bulgaria, Ecuador, Hungary, and South Korea, executives targeted the media directly by passing or enforcing laws to regulate content and packing oversight agencies with loyalists to control the media environment. Similar laws and policies empowered executives in India (1971–1975) and Sri Lanka to censor critical outlets and even expel foreign press. Indirect attacks on the media centered primarily around finance. Executives withheld state funding from critical outlets and utilized state-owned media resources for their own benefit in Bulgaria, Ecuador, Hungary, Slovenia, and Turkey. Media freedoms declined in several cases due to government harassment and intimidation. Verbal attacks against journalists and public comments questioning the press's credibility were particularly common in Hungary, Slovenia, and Turkey. Physical violence against journalists also occurred more frequently in cases like India (2000–2017) and Turkey.

As with the media, autocratizing executives across our cases sought to weaken and control civil society actors and other political opponents. For example, incumbents responded to anti-government protests with frequent arrests in India (1971–1975) and Turkey. Political opponents faced similar restrictions and arrests in cases like Ecuador, Sri Lanka, and South Korea as well. Incumbents in India (2000–2017) and South Korea also attempted to curtail civil society actors by increasing surveillance on organizations unaffiliated with the government. In Ecuador, Correa supplemented his coercion with tactics designed to co-opt opposition organizations. He offered government jobs and benefits to the leaders of these groups to divide the opposition.

Beyond the media and civil society, horizontal accountability institutions were also frequent targets in our cases. The judiciary was particularly vulnerable to attacks from the executives. Judicial independence suffered in all our cases except for South Korea. In Ecuador, Hungary, Sri Lanka, and Turkey, incumbents successfully packed the courts with loyalists or otherwise altered the legal framework to weaken the judiciary's powers. In India (1971–1975),

Gandhi struggled to weaken the judiciary substantially, but she made a few key appointments to the Supreme Court and reduced the Court's jurisdiction over some matters. Similarly, executives in Bulgaria, India (2000–2017), and Slovenia weakened judicial independence to a lesser degree than in the other cases.

Though less common than other tactics, autocratizing actors amended or replaced the constitution in over half of the cases. These instances include cases where democracy remained resilient and those that resulted in a breakdown. For example, constitutional changes occurred in matched cases, including India (1971–1975) and Sri Lanka, as well as Ecuador and Turkey. Orbán and the Fidesz amended the constitution in Hungary several times and replaced the document entirely in 2011. However, executives in the two countries matched with Hungary – South Korea and Slovenia – never made any alterations to their countries' constitutions. Likewise, constitutions in Bulgaria and India (2011–2017) remained unchanged throughout their respective episodes, despite Borisov's announced intent to do so near the end of the Bulgaria episode.

In a few of our cases, executives took more extreme or sudden actions to erode democratic institutions. Formal changes to electoral laws were uncommon among the cases, but appeared in Ecuador, Turkey, and Hungary. India (1971–1975) and Sri Lanka featured instances where incumbents postponed elections and issued a state of emergency to rule by decree, at least in parts of the country. In Slovenia, parliament substantially expanded Janša's powers during the COVID-19 pandemic, but he still faced considerable pushback from a relatively strong opposition, the judiciary, and an unsupportive public. Finally, while attacks on the judiciary were frequent, restrictions on the legislature were less common. Only executives in Ecuador and Turkey suspended the legislature. However, the limited attacks on legislative functions are perhaps unsurprising given incumbents often benefited from favorable majorities.

8.2 Resilience by Mistake

Our findings suggest that democratic resilience may often happen by mistake. In all five cases where democracy survived, leaders committed major policy blunders through economic mismanagement and corruption, prompting backlash from civil society through mass demonstrations. When faced with this crisis, leaders overestimated their popularity and underestimated institutional constraints, eventually leading to their ouster. Thus, our findings parallel recent work by Treisman (2020) showing that democratization often occurs by accident. When taken together, the evidence suggests that mistakes may help to explain both the emergence and resilience of democracy.

Ecuador and India offer the most striking examples of how miscalculations of would-be autocrats can save democracy. Among the resilient cases in our analysis, India came the closest to democratic breakdown after Gandhi resorted to extreme measures by declaring a state of emergency. In her drive to re-establish herself as a democrat and institutionalize the dictatorship, Gandhi miscalculated the extent to which the Emergency had eroded her cult of personality, eventually leading to her electoral defeat. Meanwhile, Correa struck a compromise with protestors by agreeing not to run for re-election. Given that his government removed term limits, Correa probably hoped to establish a caretaker government under Lenín Moreno and return to power in subsequent elections. However, after winning office, Moreno – whether for normative or political reasons – decided to roll back Correa's anti-democratic policies and seek corruption charges against his predecessor.

While not as dramatic, the other cases of democratic survival also saw miscalculations by leaders. Borisov and Janša lost office after corruption scandals and poor performance dogged their administrations in Bulgaria and Slovenia. For Park in South Korea, egregious corruption and criminal conspiracy with Choi Soon-sil backfired when the legislature and courts finally checked Park's excesses through impeachment and a criminal conviction.

By contrast, in most of the cases where we observe democratic breakdown, leaders were able to manage similar crisis moments or avoid them altogether, largely through narrative control and scapegoating. Unlike Correa in Ecuador, Erdoğan was willing to use lethal force to crush the Gezi Park protests, even if it meant attracting negative international media attention (Arango & Yeginsu, 2013). Meanwhile, Hungary's Orbán and India's Modi avoided a major crisis before democracy broke down. While both faced anti-government demonstrations prior to democracy's collapse, none of these demonstrations successfully reversed the autocratization episode.

One potential explanation for why some incumbents were able to circumvent or avoid major crises may stem from the use of ethnopopulist appeals as a legitimation strategy. Several of the episodes where democracies broke down featured ruling parties that espoused ethnopopulist rhetoric. For Sri Lanka (under both the SLFP and the UNP) and India (under the BJP), ruling parties adopted the racial myth of Aryan supremacy to justify executive aggrandizement at the expense of minorities, all in the name of restoring their countries to some fabled "golden age." In Turkey and Hungary, the AKP and Fidesz also promise to restore their "nations" glory by blending religious and cultural conservatism with xenophobic nationalism. In Sri Lanka, Turkey, and Hungary, this approach allowed leaders to obtain a super-majority in the parliament, while Modi's BJP has held a solid majority since taking office.

By contrast, democratic backsliding occurred under centrist leaders in four out of the five democracies that survived. While Indira Gandhi's drift toward socialism led to a major split in Congress, her ideological orientation was never radical and remained center-left (Hardgrave, 1970; Kaviraj, 1986). Her populism largely relied upon personal charisma and dynastic appeals. Meanwhile, Correa's *buen vivir* is a center-left ideology based on developmentalist social democracy with an extra emphasis on environmentalism (Caria & Domínguez, 2016). Correa engaged in technocratic populism building upon his experience as an economist and finance minister (De la Torre & Ortiz Lemos, 2016); as a result, his legitimacy largely rested on economic performance. In Bulgaria, Borisov's GERB is probably best described as a center-right (Karasimeonov, 2019); although some argue it "has no particular ideology" (V. I. Ganev, 2018, 96). Finally, South Korea's Lee and Park were center-right conservatives in their foreign policies and economic approaches, even if Park campaigned on more progressive economic policies (Chae, 2015). Only Slovenia survived an episode driven by an extremist party, and Janša certainly fits the ethnopopulist label. However, we are cautious about making any definitive claims about its resilience given that the radical right-wing SDS remains active in politics as of this writing.

While our observations about the role of ethnopopulism are limited to these cases, they nevertheless reflect earlier warnings about the negative influence of ethnonationalist extremism on democratic survival. For example, Lerner (1939, 9) warns that ideologies like fascism "create and manipulate hatreds as well as loyalties," "make use of the most deeply ingrained habits and prejudices," and "direct cruelty and despair into politically useful channels." These ideas are especially pernicious during periods of crisis, where they speak to resentment among a broad segment of society, including conservative rural dwellers, workers, and the disaffected urban middle class, by promising an alternative solution (Betz, 1993; Brustein, 1991). For this reason, democratic breakdown often originates with a disloyal opposition on the political right (Linz, 1978). The cases studied here provide additional evidence that the negative effects of ethnonationalist extremism continue to hold beyond the inter-war period.

Of course, there are contemporary examples of radical leftists claiming power only to destroy democracy from within – such as Chávez in Venezuela. Evo Morales in Bolivia (see the online appendix to this Element) also provided a unique blend of left-wing ethnopopulism, which ultimately facilitated the rise of a radical right-wing interim government and the breakdown of Bolivia's democracy. It remains to be seen whether democracy in that case will fully rebound. Conversely, the Swiss Peoples' Party (SVP) "is the strongest radical right-wing party in Western Europe," winning the most seats in every election since 2003 (Stockemer, 2018, 602). Yet, we see no evidence of democratic backsliding in Switzerland over this period, possibly due to its unique consensus-based model of government formation (Magone, 2016).

Efforts by pro-democracy actors to contain or halt executive aggrandizement may also play an important part in the story. In all five cases where democracy survived, the media exposed government mismanagement and corruption, which prompted anti-government strikes and demonstrations from civil society activists. In India, these strikes empowered the courts to rule against Indira Gandhi and convinced citizens to exercise vertical accountability through the ballot. In Ecuador, protesters forced Correa to shift strategies and abandon his attempt at a fourth-term bid. In South Korea, demonstrators re-invigorated horizontal accountability by prompting the legislature to engage in investigations that ultimately led to Park's impeachment. Despite substantial efforts at censorship and state capture, the media in Bulgaria and Slovenia played a critical role in exposing corruption, which led to mass demonstrations and electoral defeats for Janša and Borisov.

Yet, as discussed above, leaders also appear keenly aware of the potential challenge from media and civil society and attempt to contain these actors through a variety of tactics. Across all the cases in this Element, the media faced pressure from governments to censor their reporting. We found evidence of intimidation and harassment of journalists in Bulgaria, India, Turkey, and Slovenia. In Hungary, Bulgaria, and Slovenia, party loyalists purchased media houses leading to less transparency and partisan pressure on journalists to report favorably about the government. Leaders in India, Ecuador, and South Korea used defamation laws to punish journalists for reporting critical news about their governments, which likely caused others to self-censor. Civil society also faced intimidation, often in the name of national security (e.g., Ecuador, South Korea, India, and Sri Lanka). Turkey and South Korea both saw violent suppression of protests, albeit on very different scales. Refusing to register and deregistering critical civil society groups also occurs (e.g., Ecuador).

8.3 Limits of Electoral Accountability

The term executive aggrandizement conjures images of a strongman seeking to centralize authority and prolong their tenure through legal means. The episodes under Erdoğan and Correa are archetypal (Bermeo, 2016). However, our findings call into question an overly simplistic narrative of executive aggrandizement. For one, our analysis includes several episodes where *strongwomen* engaged in substantial backsliding, and although none of them oversaw a democratic breakdown, Gandhi seriously imperiled India's democracy and Bandaranaike facilitated Sri Lanka's breakdown and civil war. In addition, electoral turnover appears frequently and with somewhat unexpected results. Quite often we find multiple leaders at the helm during the episodes explored in this element. Indeed, only three episodes had a single leader – India under Gandhi, Ecuador under Correa, and Turkey under Erdoğan (de facto).

Sri Lanka illustrates the limits of electoral accountability in systems where none of the major political parties are committed to pluralism. Due to poor economic conditions and escalating confrontation with the minority Tamils, Bandaranaike experienced an electoral defeat in 1977. Unlike India after Gandhi or Ecuador after Correa, however, Sri Lanka's democracy did not recover after Bandaranaike left office. Instead, Jayewardene used his party's supermajority to rapidly dismantle the country's democratic constitution and repress minority rights, eventually leading to one of the longest-running civil wars in Asia (Bajoria, 2009).

There is also a surprising tendency for parties and leaders who engage in executive aggrandizement to experience an electoral defeat, only to have voters return them to office at a later date. Both Gandhi and Bandaranaike returned to power but did not engage in substantial autocratization during their subsequent terms. However, Gandhi's second term showed some worrying signs of possible executive aggrandizement before it was cut short when her bodyguards assassinated her in 1984 (Maiorano, 2015). In India's later episode, Vajpayee led the BJP to victory briefly in 1996 and again from 1998 to 1999, before initiating the episode in 2000. Likewise, Janša in Slovenia and Orbán in Hungary both served previous terms as prime minister before their episodes began.

Finally, several executives experienced turnovers and returned to power *during the episode*. In Bulgaria, Borisov resigned from office twice, only to have voters restore him to power via the ballot box. Janša in Slovenia initiated the episode but could not hold his early coalition together, losing office for eight years before returning to power. Similarly, in India, the BJP under Vajpayee began the episode, but then was out of office for ten years before Modi swept the 2014 polls. In each of these cases, turnovers resulted in a new government that did not engage in overt executive aggrandizement, but was also unable to implement sufficient reforms to end the episode. Once the autocratizers returned to power, they simply picked up where they left off and often with more determination than before.

Thus, our findings suggest that would-be autocrats are surprisingly resilient. They have a tendency to return to office over and over again. In some countries, their efforts are thwarted by the courts, such as Correa in Ecuador and more recently Jair Bolsonaro in Brazil. However, Orbán and Janša remind us that if the door is left open, those who return tend to learn from past mistakes. This has implications going forward for countries where leaders who previously oversaw democratic backsliding are contemplating or actively vying for leadership, such as Donald Trump in the United States (Kaufman & Haggard, 2019; Levitsky & Ziblatt, 2019).

8.4 Summary and Implications

In sum, we find that the process of executive aggrandizement tends to involve a shared set of maneuvers, with mistakes playing potentially important roles in deciding the outcome. Our cases reveal that would-be autocrats tend to fail due to their own mistakes. Civil society and media play a crucial role by alerting the population to the government's excesses, thereby activating horizontal and vertical accountability. However, executives tend to target these institutions of diagonal accountability first and across all the episodes, which may explain why so few democracies survive once executive aggrandizement begins. Furthermore, we find evidence that when ethopopulist leaders ascend to power, particularly when they secure a large majority of seats in the parliament, this tends to put democracy in severe trouble. These leaders tend to take more aggressive actions that undermine democratic institutions and practices and appear more resilient to mistakes through the use of fear and anger to obfuscate and deflect blame on minorities. Still, these findings are limited due to the small-N research design. Therefore, we conclude by reflecting on the implications of our findings for future research and policymaking.

Grappling with the ideological origins of democratic resilience and breakdown in the twenty-first century is an important area for future research. At least for now, Janša in Slovenia illustrates how extremist nationalist leaders are not entirely immune to suffering mistakes that cost them their office. There are many parallels between this case and recent episodes in the United States under Trump and Brazil under Bolsonaro. Our study did not include the latter two episodes because they were coded as ongoing at the end of 2022. Comparing Slovenia, the United States, and Brazil could yield valuable lessons about how democracies counter threats from right-wing populists, even if these cases prove to be temporary examples of democratic resilience.[12] Future research could also illuminate better the role of ideological extremism in democratic backsliding and breakdown, particularly whether right-wing parties are more pernicious than their left-wing counterparts.

---

[12] Given that all three leaders remain active in politics – with Trump actively seeking the 2024 Republican nomination as of this writing – it remains to be seen whether these cases represent true failures of right-wing populism.

Research might also help us better understand why voters support parties that have a history of engaging in anti-democratic behavior. Are failures of subsequent reformers driving an authoritarian nostalgia? Or are voters drawn back to these leaders for other reasons? Across our cases, we were surprised to find that a number of anti-democratic leaders, or at least their parties, managed to return to office after a previous electoral defeat. Hungary under Fidesz and India under the BJP illustrate this pattern. In both cases, extremist parties demonstrated their ability to learn from past mistakes and were much more effective at undermining democracy once they were returned to office. This has important implications going forward for cases where former leaders who oversaw executive accountability remain actively involved in politics, including Slovenia, the United States, and Brazil, as mentioned earlier.

For policymakers, efforts to build a robust media and civil society alongside improvements in the independence of the courts appear to be valuable investments for promoting democratic resilience. Across all the episodes explored here, we observed heroic efforts by civil society, media, and courts to check incumbents' excesses. The media and civil society were primarily responsible for informing the public about executive overreach, abuse of powers, and corruption. Their watchdog role facilitated protests and inquiries that eventually helped many democracies survive in our analysis. Thus, creative interventions that provide support to journalists, civil society actors, and the courts once backsliding is underway could help improve the odds of democratic survival.

References

Abeynaike, H. (1963). Ceylon's fiscal plight worsens as relations with the U.S. chill. *New York Times*. www.timesmachine.nytimes.com/timesmachine/1963/04/05/90569204.html?pageNumber=77

Akman, C. A., & Akçalı, P. (2017). Changing the system through instrumentalizing weak political institutions: The quest for a presidential system in Turkey in historical and comparative perspective. *Turkish Studies, 18*(4), 577–600. https://doi.org/10.1080/14683849.2017.1347508

Akyuz, K., & Hess, S. (2018). Turkey looks east: International leverage and democratic backsliding in a hybrid regime. *Mediterranean Quarterly, 29*(2), 1–26.

Albrecht, H., Koehler, K., & Schutz, A. (2021). Coup agency and prospects for democracy. *International Studies Quarterly, 65*(4), 1052–1063. https://doi.org/10.1093/isq/sqab079

Albrecht, H., Koehler, K., & Schutz, A. (2022). *Coup Agency and Mechanisms Data (CAM)*. https://militarycoups.org/#cam

Altunisik, M. B. (2005). The Turkish model and democratization in the Middle East. *Arab Studies Quarterly, 27*(1), 45–63.

Amnesty International. (2012). *The National Security Law: Curtailing Freedom of Expression and Association in the Name of Security in the Republic of Korea*. www.amnesty.org/en/wp-content/uploads/2021/06/asa250062012en.pdf

Anderson, E. (2018). Slovenian PM resigns after court ruling on referendum. *Politico*. www.politico.eu/article/miro-cerar-slovenian-pm-resigns-after-court-ruling-on-referendum/

Ankit, R. (2021). Jayaprakash Narayan and Indira Gandhi, 1966–74: Before the rivalry. *Studies in History, 37*(2), 213–234. https://doi.org/10.1177/02576430211069160

Arango, T., & Yeginsu, C. (2013). Peaceful protest over Istanbul park turns violent as police crack down. *New York Times*. www.nytimes.com/2013/06/01/world/europe/police-attack-protesters-in-istanbuls-taksim-square.html

Ayala, M., & Rochabrún, M. (2018). Ecuador votes to bring back presidential term limits. *New York Times*. www.nytimes.com/2018/02/04/world/americas/ecuador-presidential-term-limits.html

Bajomi-Lázár, P. (2013). The party colonisation of the media: The case of Hungary. *East European Politics and Societies, 27*(1), 69–89. https://doi.org/10.1177/0888325412465085

Bajoria, J. (2009). *The Sri Lankan Conflict.* Council on Foreign Affairs. www .cfr.org/backgrounder/sri-lankan-conflict

Baloch, B. A. (2021). *When Ideas Matter: Democracy and Corruption in India.* Cambridge: Cambridge University Press.

Bankuti, M., Halmai, G., & Scheppele, K. L. (2012). Hungary's illiberal turn: Disabling the constitution. *Journal of Democracy, 23*(3), 138–146.

Barrow, I. (2014). Finding the nation in assassination: The death of SWRD Bandaranaike and the assertion of a Sinhalese Sri Lankan identity. *The Historian, 76*(4), 784–802. https://doi.org/10.1111/hisn.12050

Barzachka, N. S., & Yordanova, S. P. (2020). Why Bulgaria's government has survived months of anti-corruption protests. *Washington Post.* www.washingtonpost.com/politics/2020/12/26/why-bulgarias-government-has-survived-months-anti-corruption-protests/

Basu, A. (2012). The changing fortunes of the Bharatiya Janata Party. In A. Kohli & P. Singh (Eds.), *Routledge Handbook of Indian Politics* (pp. 81–90). New York: Routledge.

Bermeo, N. (2016). On democratic backsliding. *Journal of Democracy, 27,* 5.

Bermeo, N. (2022). Questioning backsliding. *Journal of Democracy, 33*(4), 155–159.

Bernhard, M. (1993). Civil society and democratic transition in East Central Europe. *Political Science Quarterly, 108*(2), 307–326. https://doi.org/10 .2307/2152014

Bernhard, M. (2021). Democratic backsliding in Poland and Hungary. *Slavic Review, 80*(3), 585–607. https://doi.org/10.1017/slr.2021.145

Betz, H.- G. (1993). The new politics of resentment: Radical right-wing populist parties in Western Europe. *Comparative Politics, 25*(4), 413–427. https://doi.org/10.2307/422034

Bilefsky, D. (2008). Slovene leader accused of media censorship. *New York Times.* www.nytimes.com/2008/01/18/world/europe/18iht-SLOVENIA.4 .9331908.html

Boese, V. A., Edgell, A. B., Hellmeier, S., Maerz, S. F., & Lindberg, S. I. (2021). How democracies prevail: Democratic resilience as a two-stage process. *Democratization, 28*(5), 885–907. https://doi.org/10.4324/ 9781003363507-2

Boix, C. (2011). Democracy, development, and the international system. *American Political Science Review, 105*(4), 809–828. https://doi.org/10.1017/ s0003055411000402

Borders, W. (1975). Mrs. Gandhi wins court reversal of her conviction. *New York Times.* www.nytimes.com/1975/11/08/archives/mrs-gandhi-wins-court-reversal-of-her-conviction-unanimous-decision.html

Borissov, B. (2008). The Bulgarian transition towards democracy and the challenges of the new perspective. *European View*, *7*(1), 45–51. https://doi.org/10.1007/s12290-008-0032-z

Bourne, J. (1983). Notes and documents: Human rights violations in Sri Lanka. *Race & Class*, *26*(1), 111–129.

Brooke, J. (2004). Constitutional court reinstates South Korea's impeached president. *New York Times*. www.nytimes.com/2004/05/14/world/constitutional-court-reinstates-south-korea-s-impeached-president.html

Brownlee, J., & Miao, K. (2022). Why democracies survive. *Journal of Democracy*, *33*(4), 133–149. https://doi.org/10.1353/jod.2022.0052

Brustein, W. (1991). The "red menace" and the rise of Italian fascism. *American Sociological Review*, *56*(5), 652–664. https://doi.org/10.2307/2096086

Bugaric, B., & Kuhelj, A. (2015). Slovenia in crisis: A tale of unfinished democratization in East-Central Europe. *Communist and Post-Communist Studies*, *48*(4), 273–279. https://doi.org/10.1016/j.postcomstud.2015.09.003

Bukowski, C. (1999). Slovenia's transition to democracy: Theory and practice. *East European Quarterly*, *33*(1), 69.

Buultjens, R. (1982). The third world's other first lady: An interview with former Prime Minister Sirimavo Bandaranaike. *Worldview*, *21*(3), 12–17.

Cabrera, J. M. L. (2020). Ecuador's former president convicted on corruption charges. *New York Times*. www.nytimes.com/2020/04/07/world/americas/ecuador-correa-corruption-verdict.html

Cagaptay, S. (2002). The November 2002 elections and Turkey's new political era. *Middle East*, *6*(4), 43.

Camut, N. (2023). Bulgaria agrees government with rotating PMs to tackle corruption. *Politico*. www.politico.eu/article/bulgaria-finds-government-agreement-with-rotating-pm/

Caria, S., & Domínguez, R. (2016). Ecuador's buen vivir: A new ideology for development. *Latin American Perspectives*, *43*(1), 18–33. https://doi.org/10.1177/0094582x15611126

Çarkoğlu, A. (2002). Turkey's November 2002 elections: A new beginning? *Middle East Review of International Affairs*, *6*(4), 30–41.

Çarkoğlu, A. (2007). A new electoral victory for the "pro-Islamists" or the "new centre-right"? The Justice and Development Party phenomenon in the July 2007 parliamentary elections in Turkey. *South European Society & Politics*, *12*(4), 501–519. https://doi.org/10.1080/13608740701731457

Chae, H. (2015). The fluid middle in South Korean politics. *Journal of Asian and African Studies*, *50*(5), 497–519. https://doi.org/10.1177/0021909614558321

Chaibong, H. (2008). South Korea's miraculous democracy. *Journal of Democracy*, *19*, 128.

Chary, F. B. (2011). *The History of Bulgaria*. Santa Barbara, CA: Greenwood.

Choi, S.- W. (2022). Democracy and South Korea's lemon presidency. *Asian Perspective*, *46*(2), 311–341. https://doi.org/10.1353/apr.2022.0013

Çınar, M. (2018). From moderation to de-moderation: Democratic backsliding of the AKP in Turkey. In J. L. Esposito, L. Z. Rahim, & N. Ghobadzadeh (Eds.), *The Politics of Islamism: Diverging Visions and Trajectories* (pp. 127–157). Cham: Palgrave Macmillan.

Cleary, M. R., & Öztürk, A. (2022). When does backsliding lead to breakdown? uncertainty and opposition strategies in democracies at risk. *Perspectives on Politics*, *20*(1), 205–221. https://doi.org/10.1017/s1537592720003667

CNN. (2002). Bulgaria rules against ex-king. *CNN News*. www.cnn.com/2001/WORLD/europe/04/28/simeonbulgaria.court/index.html

Conaghan, C. M. (2008). Ecuador: Correa's plebiscitary presidency. *Journal of Democracy*, *19*, 46–60.

Conaghan, C. M. (2016). Ecuador under Correa. *Journal of Democracy*, *27*, 109–118. https://doi.org/10.1353/jod.2016.0040

Coppedge, M., Edgell, A. B., Knutsen, C. H., & Lindberg, S. I. (2022). *Why Democracies Develop and Decline*. New York: Cambridge University Press.

Coppedge, M., Gerring, J., Knutsen, C. H., et al. (2023). *V-Dem Country-Year Dataset v13*. Varieties of Democracy (V-Dem) Project. https://doi.org/10.23696/vdemds23

Corrales, J. (2020). Democratic backsliding through electoral irregularities. *European Review of Latin American and Caribbean Studies/Revista Europea de Estudios Latinoamericanos y del Caribe*, (109), 41–65.

Croissant, A. (2019). Beating backsliding? Episodes and outcomes of democratic backsliding in Asia-Pacific in the period 1950 to 2018. www.uni-heidelberg.de/md/politik/personal/croissant/s/croissant__2020__beating_backsliding.pdf

Dagi, I. (2008). Islamist parties and democracy: Turkey's AKP in power. *Journal of Democracy*, *19*(3), 25–30.

Dahl, R. A. (1971). *Polyarchy: Participation and Opposition*. New Haven, CT: Yale University Press.

Damar, E. (2016). Radicalisation of politics and production of new alternatives: Rethinking the secular/Islamic divide after the Gezi Park protests in Turkey. *Journal of Contemporary European Studies*, *24*(2), 207–222. https://doi.org/10.1080/14782804.2016.1167677

Daniel, F. J., & Nair, R. J. (2015). With new team in place, India's Modi tightens grip on power. *Reuters*. www.reuters.com/article/us-india-modi-insight/with-new-team-in-place-indias-modi-tightens-grip-on-power-idINK CN0IX1A320141114

De la Torre, C. (2018). Latin America's shifting politics: Ecuador after Correa. *Journal of Democracy*, *29*(4), 77–88.

De la Torre, C. (2020). Rafael Correa's technopopulism in comparative perspective. In F. Sánchez & S. Pachano (Eds.), *Assessing the Left Turn in Ecuador* (pp. 91–114). Cham: Palgrave MacMillian.

De la Torre, C., & Ortiz Lemos, A. (2016). Populist polarization and the slow death of democracy in Ecuador. *Democratization*, *23*(2), 221–241. https://doi.org/10.1080/13510347.2015.1058784

Dempsey, J. (2006). Hungary's leader, under siege over lies, refuses to resign. *New York Times*. www.nytimes.com/2006/09/20/world/europe/20hungary.html

De Silva, K. (2005). *A History of Sri Lanka*. New York: Penguin Books.

De Silva Wijeyeratne, R. (1996). Ambivalence, contingency and the failure of exclusion: The ontological schema of the 1972 constitution of the Republic of Sri Lanka. *Social & Legal Studies*, *5*(3), 365–381. https://doi.org/10.1177/096466399600500305

DeVotta, N. (2002). Illiberalism and ethnic conflict in Sri Lanka. *Journal of Democracy*, *13*, 84–98. https://doi.org/10.1353/jod.2002.0004

Dimitrova, A. L. (2022). Battered by geopolitical winds, Bulgaria struggles to restart much needed reforms. *JCMS: Journal of Common Market Studies*, *60*, 88–100. https://doi.org/10.1111/jcms.13403

Ding, I., & Slater, D. (2021). Democratic decoupling. *Democratization*, *28*(1), 63–80. https://doi.org/10.4324/9781003346395-4

Doucette, J. (2010). The terminal crisis of the "participatory government" and the election of Lee Myung Bak. *Journal of Contemporary Asia*, *40*(1), 22–43. https://doi.org/10.1080/00472330903270338

Drezov, K. (2000). Bulgaria: Transition comes full circle, 1989–1997. In G. Pridham & T. Gallagher (Eds.), *Experimenting with Democracy: Regime Change in the Balkans* (pp. 195–218). New York: Routledge.

Eckstein, H. (1975). Case studies in theory development. In F. I. Greenstein & N. W. Polsby (Eds.), *Handbook of Political Science, Volume 7: Strategies of Inquiry* (pp. 94–137). Reading, MA: Addison-Wesley.

Edgell, A. B., Maerz, S. F., Maxwell, L., et al. (2023). *Episodes of Regime Transformation Dataset (v13.0)*. Varieties of Democracy (V-Dem) Project. www.github.com/vdeminstitute/ert

Encyclopaedia Britannica. (2020). *Indira Gandhi's Impact.* www.britannica
.com/place/India/Indira-Gandhis-impact

Esen, B., & Gumuscu, S. (2017). Turkey: How the coup failed. *Journal of Democracy, 28*, 59–73. https://doi.org/10.1353/jod.2017.0006

Fackler, M. (2012). In a rowdy democracy, a dictator's daughter with an unsoiled aura. *New York Times.* www.nytimes.com/2008/07/01/world/asia/01beef.html

Fowler, B. (2004). Concentrated orange: Fidesz and the remaking of the Hungarian centre-right, 1994–2002. *Journal of Communist Studies and Transition Politics, 20*(3), 80–114. https://doi.org/10.4324/9781003060369-5

Frantz, D. (2001). Turkey: Islamists form new party. *New York Times.* www.nytimes.com/2001/08/15/world/world-briefing-europe-turkey-islamists-form-new-party.html

Frantz, D. (2002). Top Turkish candidate barred from election. *New York Times.* www.nytimes.com/2002/09/21/world/top-turkish-candidate-barred-from-election.html

Freedom House. (1993). *Freedom in the World 1993: The Annual Survey of Political Rights and Civil Liberties.* Boston, MA: National Book Network.

Freedom House. (2002). *Freedom in the World 2001–2002: The Annual Survey of Political Rights and Civil Liberties.* Washington, DC: Transaction.

Freedom House. (2003). *Freedom in the World 2003: The Annual Survey of Political Rights and Civil Liberties.* New York: Rowman & Littlefield.

Freedom House. (2005). *Freedom in the World 2005: The Annual Survey of Political Rights and Civil Liberties.* Lanham, MD: Rowman & Littlefield.

Freedom House. (2006). *Freedom in the World 2006: The Annual Survey of Political Rights and Civil Liberties.* Lanham, MD: Rowman & Littlefield.

Freedom House. (2007a). *Freedom in the World 2007: The Annual Survey of Political Rights and Civil Liberties.* Lanham, MD: Rowman & Littlefield.

Freedom House. (2007b). *Freedom of the Press 2007.* Lanham, MD: Rowman & Littlefield.

Freedom House. (2008). *Freedom in the World 2008: The Annual Survey of Political Rights and Civil Liberties.* Lanham, MD: Rowman & Littlefield.

Freedom House. (2010). *Freedom in the World 2010: The Annual Survey of Political Rights and Civil Liberties.* New York: Rowman & Littlefield.

Freedom House. (2011a). *Freedom in the World 2011: The Annual Survey of Political Rights and Civil Liberties.* Lanham, MD: Rowman & Littlefield.

Freedom House. (2011b). *Freedom of the Press 2011.* www.freedomhouse.org/sites/default/files/FOTP20201120Final20Full20Report.pdf

Freedom House. (2012). *Freedom in the World 2012: The Annual Survey of Political Rights and Civil Liberties.* Lanham, MD: Rowman & Littlefield.

Freedom House. (2013). *Freedom in the World 2013: The Annual Survey of Political Rights and Civil Liberties*. Lanham, MD: Rowman & Littlefield.

Freedom House. (2014). *Freedom in the World 2014: The Annual Survey of Political Rights and Civil Liberties*. Lanham, MD: Rowman & Littlefield.

Freedom House. (2015). *Freedom in the World 2015: The Annual Survey of Political Rights and Civil Liberties*. Lanham, MD: Rowman & Littlefield.

Freedom House. (2016). *Freedom in the World 2016: The Annual Survey of Political Rights and Civil Liberties*. Lanham, MD: Rowman & Littlefield.

Freedom House. (2017). *Freedom in the World 2017: The Annual Survey of Political Rights and Civil Liberties*. Lanham, MD: Rowman & Littlefield.

Freedom House. (2019). *Freedom in the World 2019: The Annual Survey of Political Rights and Civil Liberties*. Lanham, MD: Rowman & Littlefield.

Freedom House. (2021). *Freedom in the World 2021: Lesotho.* www.freedomhouse.org/country/lesotho/freedom-world/2021

Freedom House. (2022). *Freedom in the World 2022: Slovenia.* www.freedomhouse.org/country/slovenia/freedom-world/2022

Freedom House. (2023). *Freedom in the World 2023: Slovenia.* www.freedomhouse.org/country/slovenia/freedom-world/2023

Gamboa, L. (2022). *Resisting Backsliding: Opposition Strategies against the Erosion of Democracy*. Cambridge: Cambridge University Press.

Ganev, G., Smilov, D., & Primatarova, A. (2013). Bulgaria. In *Nations in Transit 2013*. Washington, DC: Freedom House.

Ganev, V. I. (2006). Ballots, bribes, and state building in Bulgaria. *Journal of Democracy, 17*, 75–89. https://doi.org/10.1353/jod.2006.0009

Ganev, V. I. (2018). "Soft decisionism" in Bulgaria. *Journal of Democracy, 29*, 91–103. https://doi.org/10.1353/jod.2018.0047

Ganguly, Š. (2023). Modi's undeclared emergency. *Journal of Democracy, 34*(3), 144–152. https://doi.org/10.1353/jod.0.a900326

Gençoğlu Onbaşi, F. (2016). Gezi Park protests in Turkey: From "enough is enough" to counter-hegemony? *Turkish Studies, 17*(2), 272–294. https://doi.org/10.1080/14683849.2016.1165615

George, A. L. (1979). Case studies in theory development. In P. R. Gordon (Ed.), *Diplomacy: New Approaches to History* (pp. 43–68). New York: Free Press.

George, A. L., & Bennett, A. (2005). *Case Studies and Theory Development in the Social Sciences*. Cambridge, MA: MIT Press.

Getz, A. (2022). Number of jailed journalists spikes to new global record. *Committee to Protect Journalists.* www.cpj.org/reports/2022/12/number-of-jailed-journalists-spikes-to-new-global-record/

Ghatak, M., & Roy, S. (2014). Did Gujarat's growth rate accelerate under Modi? *Economic and Political Weekly, 49*(15), 12–15.

Gherghina, S., & Bankov, P. (2023). Troublemakers and game changers: How political parties stopped democratic backsliding in Bulgaria. *Democratization, 30*(8), 1582–1603.

Gibler, D. M., & Randazzo, K. A. (2011). Testing the effects of independent judiciaries on the likelihood of democratic backsliding. *American Journal of Political Science, 55*(3), 696–709. https://doi.org/10.1111/j.1540-5907.2010.00504.x

Gijs, C., & Fota, A. (2022). Hungary's Viktor Orbán faces growing backlash over "race mixing" comments. *Politico*. www.politico.eu/article/romania-slams-hungary-viktor-orban-backlash-race-mixing-comments-unacceptable/

Ginsburg, T., & Huq, A. (2018). Democracy's near misses. *Journal of Democracy, 29*(4), 16–30. https://doi.org/10.1353/jod.2018.0059

Goeury, H. (2021). Rafael Correa's decade in power (2007–2017): Citizens' revolution, Sumak Kawsay, and neo-extractivism in Ecuador. *Latin American Perspectives, 48*(3), 206–226. https://doi.org/10.1177/0094582x211004907

Gopalakrishnan, R. (2018). Indian journalists say they intimidated, ostracized if they criticize Modi and the BJP. *Reuters*. www.reuters.com/article/us-india-politics-media-analysis/indian-journalists-say-they-intimidated-ostracized-if-they-criticize-modi-and-the-bjp-idUSKBN1HX1F4

Gottlieb, J., Blair, R., Hannah Baron, A. A., et al. (2023). *Democratic Erosion Event Dataset v6*. Democratic Erosion: A Cross-University Collaboration. www.democratic-erosion.com/event-dataset/raw-data/

Gould, H. A. (1980). The second coming: The 1980 elections in India's Hindi belt. *Asian Survey, 20*(6), 595–616.

Government of Sri Lanka. (1972). *Constitution of Sri Lanka, 1972*. www.parliament.lk/files/ca/4.%20The%20Constitution%20of%20Sri%20Lanka%20%20-%20%201972%20(Article%20105%20–134)%20Chapter%20XIII.pdf.

Gross, P. (2002). *Entangled Evolutions: Media and Democratization in Eastern Europe*. Baltimore, MD: Johns Hopkins University Press.

Guardiancich, I. (2012). The uncertain future of Slovenian exceptionalism. *East European Politics and Societies, 26*(2), 380–399. https://doi.org/10.1177/0888325411415518

Gurov, B., & Zankina, E. (2013). Populism and the construction of political charisma: Post-transition politics in Bulgaria. *Problems of Post-Communism, 60*(1), 3–17. https://doi.org/10.2753/ppc1075-8216600101

Haggard, S., & Kaufman, R. (2021). *Backsliding: Democratic Regress in the Contemporary World*. Cambridge: Cambridge University Press.

Haggard, S., & You, J.- S. (2015). Freedom of expression in South Korea. *Journal of Contemporary Asia, 45*(1), 167–179. https://doi.org/10.2139/ssrn.2505565

Hahm, S. D., & Heo, U. (2018). The first female president in South Korea: Park Geun-hye's leadership and South Korean democracy. *Journal of Asian and African Studies, 53*(5), 649–665. https://doi.org/10.1177/0021909617722376

Halmai, G. (2017). The early retirement age of Hungarian judges. In F. Nicola & B. Davies (Eds.), *EU Law Stories* (pp. 471–488). Cambridge: Cambridge University Press.

Hardgrave, R. L. (1970). The Congress in India–crisis and split. *Asian Survey, 10*(3), 256–262.

Hardgrave, R. L. (1979). India: From crisis to crisis. *Current History, 76*(446), 159–181.

Henderson, M. (1979). Setting India's democratic house in order: Constitutional amendments. *Asian Survey, 19*(10), 946–956.

Horowitz, D. L. (2000). *Ethnic Groups in Conflict*. Berkeley: University of California Press.

Hottelet, R. C. (2001). Slovenia: A small success story. *Christian Science Monitor*. www.csmonitor.com/2001/0711/p9s1.html

Huntington, S. P. (1991). How countries democratize. *Political Science Quarterly, 106*(4), 579–616. https://doi.org/10.2307/2151795

Huntington, S. P. (1993). *The Third Wave: Democratization in the Late Twentieth Century*. Norman: University of Oklahoma press.

IFES. (2018). *Republic of Ecuador Referendum, February 2018*. International Foundation for Electoral Systems. www.electionguide.org/elections/id/3082/

Inter-Parliamentary Union. (2014). *India Lok Sabha (House of People) Elections April/May 2014*. www.archive.ipu.org/parline-e/reports/2145_E.htm

Jaffrelot, C. (2015). What "Gujarat model"? – growth without development – and with socio-political polarisation. *South Asia: Journal of South Asian Studies, 38*(4), 820–838. https://doi.org/10.1080/00856401.2015.1087456

Jaffrelot, C. (2019). The fate of secularism in India. In *The BJP in Power: Indian Democracy and Religious Natonalism*. Carnegie Endowment for International Peace. www.carnegieendowment.org/2019/04/04/fate-of-secularism-in-india-pub-78689

Jenne, E. K., & Mudde, C. (2012). Can outsiders help? *Journal of Democracy, 23*, 147–155. https://doi.org/10.1353/jod.2012.0057

Joshi, R. (1975). India 1974: Growing political crisis. *Asian Survey*, *15*(2), 85–95.

Kalaycıoğlu, E. (2012). Kulturkampf in Turkey: The constitutional referendum of 12 September 2010. *South European Society and Politics*, *17*(1), 1–22. https://doi.org/10.1080/13608746.2011.600555

Karasimeonov, G. (2019). *The Party System in Bulgaria, 2009–2019.* Friedrich Ebert Stiftung. www.library.fes.de/pdf-files/bueros/sofia/15753-20191118 .pdf

Karatnycky, A., Motyl, A., & Schnetzer, A. (2002). Bulgaria. In A. Karatnycky, A. Motyl, & A. Schnetzer (Eds.), *Nations in Transit – 2001–2002: Civil Society, Democracy and Markets in East Central Europe and Newly Independent States* (pp. 129–139). New York: Routledge.

Kaufman, R. R., & Haggard, S. (2019). Democratic decline in the United States: What can we learn from middle-income backsliding? *Perspectives on Politics*, *17*(2), 417–432. https://doi.org/10.1017/s1537592718003377

Kaviraj, S. (1986). Indira Gandhi and Indian politics. *Economic and Political Weekly*, *21*(38/39), 1697–1708.

Kelemen, R. D. (2017). Europe's other democratic deficit: National authoritarianism in Europe's democratic union. *Government and Opposition*, *52*(2), 211–238. https://doi.org/10.1017/gov.2016.41

Khaitan, T. (2020). Killing a constitution with a thousand cuts: Executive aggrandizement and party-state fusion in India. *Law & Ethics of Human Rights*, *14*(1), 49–95. https://doi.org/10.2139/ssrn.3367266

Kinzer, S. (1998). Under close scrutiny, Turkey's pro-Islam party has a makeover. *New York Times*. www.nytimes.com/1998/02/26/world/under-close-scrutiny-turkey-s-pro-islam-party-has-a-makeover.html

Kodikara, S. U. (1973). Major trends in Sri Lanka's non-alignment policy after 1956. *Asian Survey*, *13*(12), 1121–1136.

Koo, H. (2002). Civil society and democracy in South Korea. *The Good Society*, *11*(2), 40–45. https://doi.org/10.1353/gso.2002.0029

Kosař, D., & Šipulová, K. (2023). Comparative court-packing. *International Journal of Constitutional Law*, *21*(1), 80–126. https://doi.org/10.1093/icon/moad012

Krašovec, A., & Johannsen, L. (2016). Recent developments in democracy in Slovenia. *Problems of Post-Communism*, *63*(5–6), 313–322. https://doi.org/ 10.1080/10758216.2016.1169932

Krašovec, A., & Lajh, D. (2021). Slovenia: Tilting the balance? In G. Verheugen, K. Vodička, & M. Brusis (Eds.), *Demokratie im Postkommunistischen EU-Raum: Erfolge, Defizite, Risiken* (pp. 161–174). Cham: Springer.

Krastev, I. (2016). What's wrong with East-Central Europe? Liberalism's failure to deliver. *Joural of Democracy, 27*, 35–38.

Krekó, P., & Enyedi, Z. (2018). Orbán's laboratory of illiberalism. *Journal of Democracy, 29*(3), 39–51. https://doi.org/10.1353/jod.2018.0043

Laebens, M. G., & Lührmann, A. (2021). What halts democratic erosion? The changing role of accountability. *Democratization, 28*(5), 908–928. https://doi.org/10.1080/13510347.2021.1897109

Lancaster, C. (2014). The iron law of Erdogan: The decay from intra-party democracy to personalistic rule. *Third World Quarterly, 35*(9), 1672–1690. https://doi.org/10.1080/01436597.2014.970866

Leepson, M. (1976). India under authoritarian rule. *Editorial Research Reports*. www.library.cqpress.com/cqresearcher/document.php?id=cqresrre 1976061100

Leidig, E. (2020). Hindutva as a variant of right-wing extremism. *Patterns of Prejudice, 54*(3), 215–237. https://doi.org/10.1080/0031322x.2020 .1759861

Leidig, E., & Mudde, C. (2023). Bharatiya Janata Party (BJP): The overlooked populist radical right party. *Journal of Language and Politics, 22*, 360–377. https://doi.org/10.1075/jlp.22134.lei

Lerner, M. (1939). The pattern of dictatorship. In G. S. Ford (Ed.), *Dictatorship in the Modern World* (pp. 3–21). London: University of Minnesota Press.

Levitsky, S., & Ziblatt, D. (2019). *How Democracies Die*. New York: Crown.

Lijphart, A. (1971). Comparative politics and the comparative method. *American Political Science Review, 65*(3), 682–693.

Lijphart, A. (1977). *Democracy in Plural Societies: A Comparative Exploration*. New Haven, CT: Yale University Press.

Linz, J. J. (1978). *The Breakdown of Democratic Regimes: Crisis, Breakdown, and Reequilibration*. Baltimore, MD: Johns Hopkins University Press.

Linz, J. J., & Stepan, A. (1996). Toward consolidated democracies. *Journal of Democracy, 7*(2), 14–33.

Lipset, S. M. (1959). Some social requisites of democracy: Economic development and political legitimacy. *American Political Science Review, 53*(1), 69–105. https://doi.org/10.2307/1951731

Lott, L. (2023). Academic freedom growth and decline episodes. *Higher Education*, 1–19. https://doi.org/10.1007/s10734-023-01156-z.

Lovec, M. (2017). *Nations in Transit 2017: Slovenia*. Freedom House. www .freedomhouse.org/country/slovenia/nations-transit/2017

Lovec, M. (2018). *Nations in Transit 2018: Slovenia*. Freedom House. www .freedomhouse.org/country/slovenia/nations-transit/2018

Lovec, M. (2021). *Nations in Transit 2021: Slovenia.* Freedom House. www .freedomhouse.org/country/slovenia/nations-transit/2021

Lührmann, A. (2021). Disrupting the autocratization sequence: Towards democratic resilience. *Democratization, 28*(5), 1017–1039.

Lührmann, A., & Lindberg, S. I. (2019). A third wave of autocratization is here: What is new about it? *Democratization, 26*(7), 1095–1113. https://doi.org/ 10.1080/13510347.2019.1582029

Lührmann, A., Tannenberg, M., & Lindberg, S. I. (2018). Regimes of the world (row): Opening new avenues for the comparative study of political regimes. *Politics and Governance, 6*(1), 60–77.

Maerz, S. F., Edgell, A. B., Wilson, M. C., Hellmeier, S., & Lindberg, S. I. (2023). Episodes of regime transformation. *Journal of Peace Research,* 1–18. https://doi.org/10.1177/00223433231168192

Maerz, S. F., & Schneider, C. Q. (2020). Comparing public communication in democracies and autocracies: Automated text analyses of speeches by heads of government. *Quality & Quantity, 54*(2), 517–545. https://doi.org/10.1007/ s11135-019-00885-7

Magone, J. (2016). *The Statecraft of Consensus Democracies in a Turbulent World: A Comparative Study of Austria, Belgium, Luxembourg, the Netherlands and Switzerland.* New York: Routledge.

Mainwaring, S., & Masoud, T. E. (2022). *Democracy in Hard Places.* Oxford: Oxford University Press.

Maiorano, D. (2015). *Autumn of the Matriarch: Indira Gandhi's Final Term in Office.* Oxford: Oxford University Press.

Malhotra, I. (1989). *Indira Gandhi: A Personal and Political Biography.* Boston, MA: Northeastern University Press.

Marquand, R., & Bowers, F. (1994). Slovenian premier urges West: Stay tough on Serbs. *Christian Science Monitor.* www.csmonitor.com/1994/ 0408/08062.html

Mashal, M., & Kumar, H. (2024). Lights! Camera! Modi! It's a one-man show on Indian television. *New York Times.* www.nytimes.com/2024/02/03/world/ asia/india-modi-ayodhya-media.html

Mazzuca, S. L. (2013). The rise of rentier populism. *Journal of Democracy, 24*(2), 108–122. https://doi.org/10.1353/jod.2013.0034

McCurry, J. (2017). South Korea spy agency admits trying to rig 2012 presidential election. *The Guardian.* www.theguardian.com/world/2017/aug/04/ south-koreas-spy-agency-admits-trying-rig-election-national-intelligence-service-2012

McFadden, R. D. (2018). Atal Bihari Vajpayee, former prime minister of India, dies at 93. *New York Times*. www.nytimes.com/2018/08/16/obituaries/atal-bihari-vajpayee-dead.html

Mehta, P. B. (2007). India's unlikely democracy: The rise of judicial sovereignty. *Journal of Democracy, 18*(2), 70–83. https://doi.org/10.1353/jod.2007.0030

Melone, A. P. (1996). The struggle for judicial independence and the transition toward democracy in Bulgaria. *Communist and Post-Communist Studies, 29*(2), 231–243. https://doi.org/10.1016/s0967-067x(96)80007-9

Mendelsohn, O. (1978). The collapse of the Indian National Congress. *Pacific Affairs, 51*(1), 41–66.

Milacic, F. (2022). Stateness and democratic backsliding in the former Yugoslavia: How political actors subvert democracy in the name of the nation. *Nations and Nationalism, 28*(4), 1474–1493. https://doi.org/10.1111/nana.12861

Mitra, S. K. (1992). Democracy and political change in India. *Journal of Commonwealth & Comparative Politics, 30*(1), 9–38.

Mussells, P. M. (1980). *Democracy and Emergency Rule in India: Political Change under Mrs. Gandhi* (Doctoral dissertation, University of Oklahoma). www.proquest.com/docview/288341265/3FC83767997B422DPQ

Mustafi, S. M. (2013). What makes Narendra Modi a middle-class hero? *New York Times*. www.archive.nytimes.com/india.blogs.nytimes.com/2013/05/16/what-makes-narendra-modi-a-middle-class-hero/

New York Times. (2008a). Exit polls show opposition leading in Slovenia elections. *International Herald Tribune*. www.nytimes.com/2008/09/21/world/europe/21iht-slovenia.4.16347697.html

New York Times. (2008b). South Korea cracks down on protestors. *New York Times*. www.nytimes.com/2008/07/01/world/asia/01beef.html

Nilsen, A. G. (2018). India's turn to rights-based legislation (2004–2014): A critical review of the literature. *Social Change, 48*(4), 653–665. https://doi.org/10.1177/0049085718800861

Noutcheva, G., & Bechev, D. (2008). The successful laggards: Bulgaria and romania's accession to the EU. *East European Politics and Societies, 22*(1), 114–144.

Novak, M., & Lajh, D. (2023). Challenges facing organised interests under a populist right-wing government in Slovenia. *Politics and Governance, 11*(1), 28–38. https://doi.org/10.17645/pag.v11i1.5859

Oltay, E. (2006). Hungarian opposition party locked in power struggle with the government. *Comparative Southeast European Studies, 54*(4), 474–497. https://doi.org/10.1515/soeu-2006-540403

Onbaşı, N. (2020). The role of populist strategies in differing outcomes of corruption scandals in Brazil and Turkey. *Turkish Studies, 21*(2), 188–207. https://doi.org/10.1080/14683849.2019.1619175

OSCE. (2014). *Hungary Parliamentary Elections, 6 April 2014: OSCE/ ODIHR Limited Election Observation Mission Report.* www.osce.org/files/f/ documents/c/0/121098.pdf

OSCE. (2018). *Hungary Parliamentary Elections, 6 April 2018: OSCE/ODIHR Limited Election Observation Mission Final Report.* www.osce.org/files/f/ documents/0/9/385959.pdf

Över, D. (2021). Democratic backsliding and the media: The convergence of news narratives in Turkey. *Media, Culture & Society, 43*(2), 343–358. https: //doi.org/10.1177/0163443720975879

Özbudun, E. (2014). AKP at the crossroads: Erdoğan's majoritarian drift. *South European Society and Politics, 19*(2), 155–167. https://doi.org/10 .1080/13608746.2014.920571

Ozturk, O. (2021). Democratic erosion in India: A case study. *Democratic Erosion Consortium.* www.democratic-erosion.com/2021/02/05/ democratic-erosion-in-india-a-case-study/

Pai, S. (1996). Transformation of the Indian party system: The 1996 Lok Sabha elections. *Asian Survey, 36*(12), 1170–1183. https://doi.org/10.2307/ 2645573

Palmer, N. D. (1977). India in 1976: The politics of depolticization. *Asian Survey, 17*(2), 160–180. https://doi.org/10.2307/2643474

Park, J.- M., & Kim, J. (2016). South Korean parliament votes overwhelmingly to impeach President Park. *Reuters.* www.reuters.com/article/us-southkorea-politics/south-korean-parliament-votes-overwhelmingly-to-impeach-presid ent-park-idUSKBN13X2JS

Park, R. L. (1975). Political crisis in India, 1975. *Asian Survey, 15*(11), 996–1013. https://doi.org/10.2307/2643553

Patil, T. (2017). The politics of race, nationhood and Hindu nationalism: The case of Gujarat riots of 2002. *Asian Journal of Social Science, 45*(1–2), 27–54. https://doi.org/10.1163/15685314-04501002

Pelke, L., & Croissant, A. (2021). Conceptualizing and measuring autocratization episodes. *Swiss Political Science Review, 27*(2), 434–448. https: //doi.org/10.1111/spsr.12437

Petrequin, S. (2022). Exiled ex-Ecuador president doesn't exclude political return. *Associated Press.* www.apnews.com/article/immigration-migration-europe-belgium-ecuador-c0f7db75cdc1fcd3f93b4c633808a6ac

Pirro, A. L., & Stanley, B. (2022). Forging, bending, and breaking: Enacting the "illiberal playbook"' in Hungary and Poland. *Perspectives on Politics, 20*(1), 86–101. https://doi.org/10.1017/s1537592721001924

Plys, K. V. M. (2020). *Brewing Resistance: Indian Coffee House and the Emergency in Postcolonial India*. Cambridge: Cambridge University Press.

Przeworski, A. (2000). *Democracy and Development: Political Institutions and Well-Being in the World, 1950–1990*. New York: Cambridge University Press.

Przeworski, A., & Limongi, F. (1997). Modernization: Theories and facts. *World Politics, 49*(2), 155–183. https://doi.org/10.1353/wp.1997.0004

Rabushka, A. (1972). *Politics in Plural Societies*. Columbus, OH: Charles E. Merrill.

Racz, B. (1991). Political pluralisation in Hungary: The 1990 elections. *Soviet Studies, 43*(1), 107–136. https://doi.org/10.1080/09668139108411913

Racz, B. (2003). The left in Hungary and the 2002 parliamentary elections. *Europe-Asia Studies, 55*(5), 747–769. https://doi.org/10.1080/0966813032000086864

Raj, S. (2023). New Indian textbooks purged of Muslim history and Hindu extremism. *New York Times*. www.nytimes.com/2023/04/06/world/asia/india-textbooks-changes.html

Rangnekar, D. (1960). The nationalist revolution in Ceylon. *Pacific Affairs, 33*(4), 361–374. https://doi.org/10.2307/2753395

Reenock, C., Staton, J. K., & Radean, M. (2013). Legal institutions and democratic survival. *The Journal of Politics, 75*(2), 491–505. https://doi.org/10.1017/s0022381613000169

Renwick, A. (2006). Why Hungary and Poland differed in 1989: The role of medium-term frames in explaining the outcomes of democratic transition. *Democratisation, 13*(1), 36–57. https://doi.org/10.1080/13510340500378233

Reporters Without Borders. (2023). *World Press Freedom Index*. www.rsf.org/en/index

Reuters. (1996). *Supporters Mob the Bulgarian King on His Return*. www.timesmachine.nytimes.com/timesmachine/1996/05/27/077615.html?pageNumber=4

Rizman, R. M. (1999). Radical right politics in Slovenia. In S. P. Ramet (Ed.), *The Radical Right in Central and Eastern Europe since 1989* (pp. 147–170). University Park, PA: Penn State Press.

Rizman, R. M. (2006). *Uncertain Path: Democratic Transition and Consolidation in Slovenia*. College Station: Texas A&M University Press.

Rosenberg, T. (1998). Is Viktor Orban too old to lead Hungary? *New York Times*. www.nytimes.com/1998/06/27/opinion/editorial-observer-is-viktor-orban-too-old-to-lead-hungary.html

Ruparelia, S. (2006). Rethinking institutional theories of political moderation: The case of Hindu nationalism in India, 1996–2004. *Comparative Politics*, 317–336. https://doi.org/10.2307/20434000

Ruparelia, S. (2013). India's new rights agenda: Genesis, promises, risks. *Pacific Affairs*, *86*(3), 569–590. https://doi.org/10.5509/2013863569

Rupnik, J. (2012). Hungary's illiberal turn: How things went wrong. *Journal of Democracy*, *23*, 132–137. https://doi.org/10.1353/jod.2012.0051

Rupnik, J. (2022). Orbán's Hungary: From "illiberal democracy" to the authoritarian temptation. In A. Dieckhoff, C. Jaffrelot, & E. Massicard (Eds.), *Contemporary Populists in Power* (pp. 133–152). Cham: Palgrave MacMillan.

Samarasinghe, S. d. A. (1983). Sri Lanka in 1982: A year of elections. *Asian Survey*, 158–164. https://doi.org/10.2307/2644347

Sanchez-Sibony, O. (2017). Classifying Ecuador's regime under Correa: A procedural approach. *Journal of Politics in Latin America*, *9*(3), 121–140. https://doi.org/10.1177/1866802x1700900305

Sang-Hun, C. (2007). Former Seoul mayor wins South Korean presidential nomination. *New York Times*. www.nytimes.com/2007/08/20/world/asia/20iht-korea.1.7181734.html

Sang-Hun, C. (2016). Park Geun-hye was accomplice in extortion, South Korean prosecutors say. *New York Times*. www.nytimes.com/2013/05/13/world/asia/south-korea-seeks-arrest-of-podcaster-choo-chin-woo.html

Sang-Hun, C. (2017). South Korea removes President Park Geun-hye. *New York Times*. www.nytimes.com/2017/03/09/world/asia/park-geun-hye-impeached-south-korea.html

Saraçoğlu, C., & Demirkol, Ö. (2015). Nationalism and foreign policy discourse in Turkey under the AKP rule: Geography, history and national identity. *British Journal of Middle Eastern Studies*, *42*(3), 301–319. https://doi.org/10.1080/13530194.2014.947152

Sarfati, Y. (2015). Dynamics of mobilization during Gezi Park protests in Turkey. In I. Epstein (Ed.), *The Whole World Is Texting: Youth Protest in the Information Age* (pp. 25–43). Leiden: Brill.

Sartori, G. (1970). Concept misformation in comparative politics. *American Political Science Review*, *64*(4), 1033–1053. https://doi.org/10.2307/1958356

Sato, Y., Lundstedt, M., Morrison, K., Boese, V. A., & Lindberg, S. I. (2022). Institutional order in episodes of autocratization. *V-Dem Working Paper*, *133*.

Scheppele, K. L. (2018). Autocratic legalism. *The University of Chicago Law Review*, *85*(2), 545–584.

Scheppele, K. L. (2022). How Viktor Orbán wins. *Journal of Democracy*, *33*(3), 45–61. https://doi.org/10.1353/jod.2022.0039

Schmall, E., & Yasir, S. (2021). "Are we human?" Modi's use of antiterror law draws scrutiny from courts. *New York Times*. www.nytimes.com/2021/10/12/world/asia/modi-india-antiterror-law.html

Schumpeter, J. A. (1942). *Capitalism, Socialism and Democracy*. New York: Harper & Brothers.

Seawright, J., & Gerring, J. (2008). Case selection techniques in case study research: A menu of qualitative and quantitative options. *Political Research Quarterly*, *61*(2), 294–308. https://doi.org/10.1177/1065912907313077

Selçuk, O. (2016). Strong presidents and weak institutions: Populism in Turkey, Venezuela and Ecuador. *Southeast European and Black Sea Studies*, *16*(4), 571–589. https://doi.org/10.1080/14683857.2016.1242893

Sezgin, Y. (2018). Resiliency and pitfalls of crisis regimes: Reimagining the future of Turkey's democracy through the lens of the Indian emergency. *Review of Middle East Studies*, *52*(1), 54–65. https://doi.org/10.1017/rms.2018.11

Simmons, M. (1997). They'll give the king anything except a crown. *New York Times*. www.timesmachine.nytimes.com/timesmachine/1999/11/24/580473.html?pageNumber=4

Singh, I. B. (1980). The Indian mass media system: Before, during and after the national emergency. *Canadian Journal of Communication*, *7*(2), 38–49. https://doi.org/10.22230/cjc.1980v7n2a248

Slater, D., & Wong, J. (2013). The strength to concede: Ruling parties and democratization in developmental Asia. *Perspectives on Politics*, *11*(3), 717–733. https://doi.org/10.1017/s1537592713002090

Smilov, D. (2008). Bulgaria. In G. Mesežnikov, O. Gyárfášová, & D. Smilov (Eds.), *Populist Politics and Liberal Democracy in Central and Eastern Europe* (pp. 13–36). Bratislava: IVO (IPA).

Sohn, Y., & Kang, W.- T. (2013). South Korea in 2012: An election year under rebalancing challenges. *Asian Survey*, *53*(1), 198–205. https://doi.org/10.1525/as.2013.53.1.198

Spirova, M. (2015). Bulgaria. In *Nations in Transit 2017*. Washington, DC: Freedom House.

Spirova, M. (2017). Bulgaria. In *Nations in Transit 2017*. Washington, DC: Freedom House.

State Department. (2002). *Bulgaria 2002 Human Rights Report*. www.state.gov/g/drl/rls/hrrpt/2002/18358pf.htm

Sterling, C. (1975). Rule of 600 million– and alone. *New York Times*. Retrieved from www.nytimes.com/1975/08/10/archives/ruler-of-600-million-and-alone-indira-gandhi-is-unmaking-a.html

Stockemer, D. (2018). The rising tide: Local structural determinants of the radical right-wing vote in Switzerland. *Comparative European Politics*, *16*, 602–619. https://doi.org/10.1057/s41295-016-0087-1

Stoyan, A. T. (2020). Ambitious reform via constituent assemblies: Determinants of success in contemporary Latin America. *Studies in Comparative International Development*, *55*(1), 99–121. https://doi.org/10.1007/s12116-019-09297-y

Stuenkel, O. (2019). Is Ecuador a model for post-populist democratic recovery? *Carnegie Endowment for International Peace*. www.carnegieendowment.org/2019/07/11/is-ecuador-model-for-post-populist-democratic-recovery-pub-79472

Szikra, D. (2014). Democracy and welfare in hard times: The social policy of the Orbán Government in Hungary between 2010 and 2014. *Journal of European Social Policy*, *24*(5), 486–500. https://doi.org/10.1177/0958928714545446

Szikra, D., & Öktem, K. G. (2023). An illiberal welfare state emerging? Welfare efforts and trajectories under democratic backsliding in Hungary and Turkey. *Journal of European Social Policy*, *33*(2), 201–215. https://doi.org/10.1177/09589287221141365

Tagliabue, J. (2001). On top in Bulgaria: New premier is the old king. *New York Times*. www.timesmachine.nytimes.com/timesmachine/2001/07/13/225665.html?pageNumber=4

Taş, H. (2015). Turkey–from tutelary to delegative democracy. *Third World Quarterly*, *36*(4), 776–791. https://doi.org/10.1080/01436597.2015.1024450

Teorell, J. (2010). *Determinants of Democratization: Explaining Regime Change in the World, 1972–2006*. New York: Cambridge University Press.

Tepe, S. (2005). Turkey's AKP: A model "Muslim-Democratic" party? *Journal of Democracy*, *16*(3), 69–82. https://doi.org/10.1353/jod.2005.0053

Thapar, R. (1996). The theory of Aryan race and India: History and politics. *Social scientist*, *24*(1–3), 3–29. https://doi.org/10.2307/3520116

Time. (1960). Ceylon: Tearful ruler. *Time Magazine*. www.content.time.com/time/subscriber/article/0,33009,869666,00.html

Time. (1969). India: The lady v. the Syndicate. *Time Magazine*. www.content.time.com/time/subscriber/article/0,33009,901293-1,00.html

Tomini, L. (2021). Don't think of a wave! A research note about the current autocratization debate. *Democratization, 28*(6), 1191–1201. https://doi.org/10.1080/13510347.2021.1874933

Travelli, A. (2023). India's top court clears way for Rahul Gandhi's return to parliament. *New York Times.* www.nytimes.com/2023/08/04/world/asia/india-rahul-gandhi-defamation.html

Treisman, D. (2020). Democracy by mistake: How the errors of autocrats trigger transitions to freer government. *American Political Science Review, 114*(3), 792–810. https://doi.org/10.1017/s0003055420000180

Tudor, M. (2023). Why India's democracy is dying. *Journal of Democracy, 34*(3), 121–132. https://doi.org/10.1353/jod.0.a900324

Tully, M. (2002). Vajpayee reveals his true colors. *CNN News.* www.edition.cnn.com/2002/WORLD/asiapcf/south/04/18/india.vajpayee/index.html

Türk, H. B. (2018). "Populism as a medium of mass mobilization": The case of Recep Tayyip Erdoğan. *International Area Studies Review, 21*(2), 150–168. https://doi.org/10.1177/2233865918761111

Tworzecki, H. (2019). Poland: A case of top-down polarization. *The Annals of the American Academy of Political and Social Science, 681*(1), 97–119. https://doi.org/10.1177/0002716218809322

Ueda, T. (2019). Who appoints judges? Judicial independence and democratisation of the judiciary in India. In T. Yamamoto & T. Ueda (Eds.), *Law and Democracy in Contemporary India: Constitution, Contact Zone, and Performing Rights* (pp. 51–83). Cham: Palgrave MacMillan.

UNESCO. (2023). Statistics on killed journalists. *Observatory of Killed Journalists.* www.unesco.org/en/safety-journalists/observatory/statistics?hub=72609

Vaishnav, M. (2021). The challenge of India's democratic backsliding. *Democracy: A Journal of Ideas.* www.democracyjournal.org/magazine/62-special-issue/the-challenge-of-indias-democratic-backsliding/

Varol, O. O., Dalla Pellegrina, L., & Garoupa, N. (2017). An empirical analysis of judicial transformation in Turkey. *The American Journal of Comparative Law, 65*(1), 187–216. https://doi.org/10.1093/ajcl/avx013

Varshney, A. (2022). How India's ruling party erodes democracy. *Journal of Democracy, 33*(4), 104–118. https://doi.org/10.1353/jod.2022.0050

Venugopal, R. (2015). Democracy, development and the executive presidency in Sri Lanka. *Third World Quarterly, 36*(4), 670–690. https://doi.org/10.1080/01436597.2015.1024400

Waldman, A. (2002). Hopes and fears in India stirred by Hindu nationalist. *New York Times.* www.timesmachine.nytimes.com/timesmachine/2002/12/15/398926.html?pageNumber=21

Waldman, A. (2004). In huge upset, Gandhi's party wins election in India. *New York Times*. www.nytimes.com/2004/05/13/international/asia/in-huge-upset-gandhis-party-wins-election-in-india.html

Waldner, D., & Lust, E. (2018). Unwelcome change: Coming to terms with democratic backsliding. *Annual Review of Political Science, 21*, 93–113. https://doi.org/10.1146/annurev-polisci-050517-114628

Warnapala, W. (1979). Sri Lanka 1978: Reversal of policies and strategies. *Asian Survey, 9*(2), 178–190. https://doi.org/10.2307/2643784

Warnapala, W. (1983). Seeking sanction for dictatorship: The referendum in sri lanka. *Economic and Political Weekly, 18*(1/2), 17–19.

Weiner, M. (1977). The 1977 parliamentary elections in India. *Asian Survey, 17*(7), 619–626. https://doi.org/10.2307/2643409

Weinraub, B. (1974). India's rail strike ends in collapse. *New York Times*. www.nytimes.com/1974/05/28/archives/indias-rail-strike-ends-in-collapse.html

Welsh, D. (1993). Domestic politics and ethnic conflict. *Survival, 35*(1), 63–80. https://doi.org/10.1080/00396339308442674

Whitney, C. R. (1997). Now a tightrope walker: Bulgaria's toppled king. *New York Times*. www.timesmachine.nytimes.com/timesmachine/1997/01/31/447935.html?pageNumber=12

Wickramasinghe, N. (2012). Democracy and entitlements in Sri Lanka: The 1970s crisis over university admission. *South Asian History and Culture, 3*(1), 81–96. https://doi.org/10.1080/19472498.2012.639521

Wien, M. (2021). Remembrance of the monarchy as a factor in Bulgarian politics. In B. A. John Paul Newman (Ed.), *Balkan Legacies: The Long Shadow of Conflict and Ideological Experiment in Southeastern Europe* (pp. 275–292). West Lafayette, IN: Purdue University Press.

Wilson, M. C., Edgell, A. B., Sato, Y., Boese-Schlosser, V., & Lindberg, S. I. (2024). Autocratization – not an "illiberal turn." In M. Laruelle (Ed.), *Oxford Handbook of Illiberalism*. New York: Oxford University Press. https://doi.org/10.1093/oxfordhb/9780197639108.013.20.

Wriggins, W. H. (1981). Sri Lanka in 1980: The year of constraints. *Asian Survey, 21*(2), 203–211. https://doi.org/10.2307/2643765

Yavuz, M. H. (2009). *Secularism and Muslim Democracy in Turkey*. Cambridge: Cambridge University Press.

Yilmaz, I., & Bashirov, G. (2018). The AKP after 15 years: Emergence of Erdoganism in Turkey. *Third World Quarterly, 39*(9), 1812–1830. https://doi.org/10.1080/01436597.2018.1447371

Yovcheva, T., & Bértoa, F. C. (2023). Bulgaria is stuck in an electoral doom loop. *Foreign Policy*. www.foreignpolicy.com/2023/03/31/bulgaria-election-parliament-president-radev-putin-russia-ukraine-polarization/

Zankina, E., & Gurov, B. (2018). Bulgaria. In *Nations in Transit 2018*. Washington, DC: Freedom House.

Acknowledgements

Funding from the University of Alabama Department of Political Science and College of Arts and Sciences supported this research. The authors also wish to extend their appreciation to Waleed Hazbun for providing financial support through the Program on the Middle East in Global Affairs. We are grateful for feedback from Emily Beaulieu Bacchus at the Southern Political Science Association annual meeting in January 2023 and Jennifer McCoy at the American Political Science Association meeting in September 2023. Panelists and participants at both conferences also provided valuable insights that helped improve the research design and overall manuscript. Prince Selorm Tetteh provided research assistance in the final stages of the project. Finally, we are grateful to Michael Bernhard for suggesting we consider publishing this research as an Element. The authors contributed equally to the preparation of this Element. All errors and omissions are our own.

Cambridge Elements ≡

Political Economy

David Stasavage
New York University

David Stasavage is Julius Silver Professor in the Wilf Family Department of Politics at New York University. He previously held positions at the London School of Economics and at Oxford University. His work has spanned a number of different fields and currently focuses on two areas: development of state institutions over the long run and the politics of inequality. He is a member of the American Academy of Arts and Sciences.

About the Series

The Element Series Political Economy provides authoritative contributions on important topics in the rapidly growing field of political economy. Elements are designed so as to provide broad and in-depth coverage combined with original insights from scholars in political science, economics, and economic history. Contributions are welcome on any topic within this field.

Cambridge Elements ≡

Political Economy

Elements in the Series

A full series listing is available at: www.cambridge.org/EPEC

For EU product safety concerns, contact us at Calle de José Abascal, 56–1°,
28003 Madrid, Spain or eugpsr@cambridge.org.